EYEWITNESS
WORLD
WAR II

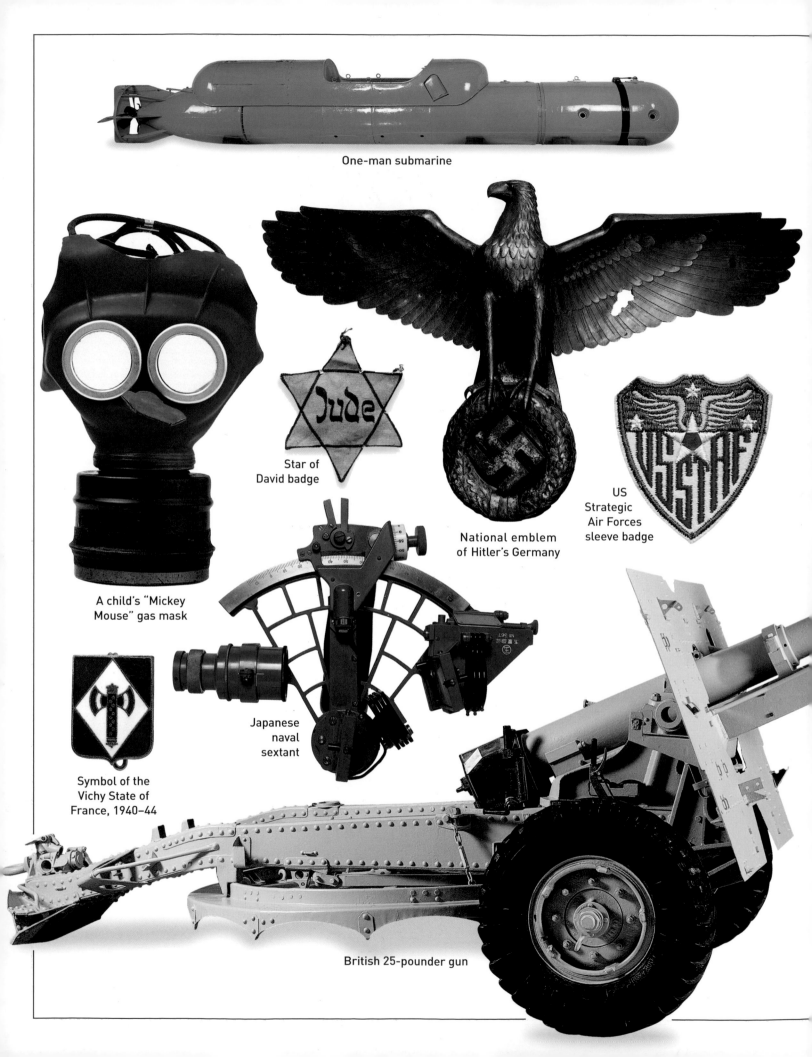

One-man submarine

A child's "Mickey Mouse" gas mask

Star of David badge

National emblem of Hitler's Germany

US Strategic Air Forces sleeve badge

Symbol of the Vichy State of France, 1940–44

Japanese naval sextant

British 25-pounder gun

Polish medal

EYEWITNESS
WORLD
WAR II

Russian medal

Written by
SIMON ADAMS

Photographed by
ANDY CRAWFORD

DK

Beretta pistol
owned by the
Italian viceroy
of Ethiopia

DK | Penguin Random House

Project editor Melanie Halton
Senior art editor Jane Tetzlaff
Art editor Ann Cannings
Assistant editor Jayne Miller
Managing editor Sue Grabham
Senior managing art editor Julia Harris
Additional photography Steve Gorton
Production Kate Oliver
Picture research Mollie Gillard
Senior DTP designer Andrew O'Brien

RELAUNCH EDITION (DK UK)
Editor Ashwin Khurana
US editor Margaret Parrish
Senior designers Rachael Grady, Spencer Holbrook
Managing editor Gareth Jones
Managing art editor Philip Letsu
Publisher Andrew Macintyre
Producer, preproduction Adam Stoneham
Senior producer Charlotte Cade
Jacket editor Maud Whatley
Jacket designer Laura Brim
Jacket design development manager Sophia MTT
Publishing director Jonathan Metcalf
Associate publishing director Liz Wheeler
Art director Phil Ormerod

RELAUNCH EDITION (DK INDIA)
Editor Surbhi Nayyar Kapoor
Art editor Deep Shikha Walia
Senior DTP designer Harish Aggarwal
DTP designers Anita Yadav, Pawan Kumar
Managing editor Alka Thakur Hazarika
Managing art editor Romi Chakraborty
CTS manager Balwant Singh
Jacket editorial manager Saloni Talwar
Jacket designers Govind Mittal, Suhita Dharamjit, Vikas Chauhan

First American Edition, 2000
This American Edition, 2014
Published in the United States by DK Publishing
1450 Broadway, Suite 801
New York, NY 10018

19 10 9 8
026-196563—07/14

A catalog record for this book is available from
the Library of Congress.

ISBN 978-1-4654-2059-6 (Paperback)
ISBN 978-1-4654-2101-2 (ALB)

DK books are available at special discounts when
purchased in bulk for sales promotions, premiums,
fund-raising, or educational use. For details, contact:
DK Publishing Special Markets, 1450 Broadway, Suite
801, New York, NY 10018 or SpecialSale@dk.com.

Color reproduction by Alta Image Ltd., London, UK
Printed in China
A WORLD OF IDEAS:
SEE ALL THERE IS TO KNOW

www.dk.com

Model of Nazi
standard bearer

British beach mine

Air-raid rattle

British fire service badge

Straw snow boots made by
German soldiers in Russia

Japanese prayer flag

Contents

Evacuation
card game

A world divided

In the early 20th century, the world was split into three main camps: democratic nations—including Britain, France, the Netherlands, Czechoslovakia, Belgium, and the US—where people elected their governments; nations ruled by dictators—including fascist Italy, Nazi Germany, and nationalist Japan; and the Communist state—the Soviet Union (USSR)—meant to be run by workers but in fact run by the tyrannical Josef Stalin. Conflicts between these three camps led to a world war in 1939.

Power to workers
Communists, who were against private ownership, took power in Russia in 1917 to form the Soviet Union. Few countries trusted it or its leader, and refused to support Soviet beliefs.

Hammer

Sickle

Soviet symbol
The hammer (for industrial workers) and sickle (for farm workers) was the Soviet Union's symbol and was on the nation's flag.

Stainless-steel figures are young, strong, and attractive

Vera Mukhina's Worker and Peasant statue, for the Paris World Fair, 1937

Spread of Fascism
In 1922, Benito Mussolini turned Italy into a fascist (dictator-led) state. By the 1930s, fascist rulers ran Spain, Portugal, Austria, Romania, and Germany—where the Nazi Party took fascist ideas to the extreme.

Italian Fascist Youth march

Blue-bordered royal coat of arms

Italian Fascism
Italian fascists used the fasces (an ancient Romam symbol of power) as their symbol. But Italy remained a kingdom, so its flag bore the royal coat of arms.

Imperial
Japanese
army uniform,
c. 1930s

Nazi Nation symbol

The swastika is an ancient religious symbol, common in Greece and India. Adolf Hitler adopted the swastika as the symbol for the Nazi Party, and it appeared on the German national flag in 1935.

"After 15 years of despair, a great people is back on its feet."

ADOLF HITLER, 1933

Presentation box for a copy of Mein Kampf

Nazi Party membership book

Imperial Japan

Japan fought on the side of Britain, France, and the US in World War I, but felt cheated when given little new territory. In the 1920s, nationalists came to rule Japan, wanting to make it an imperial power in Asia.

Hitler's proposals

Hitler wrote *Mein Kampf* (*My Struggle*) in 1924. It was ignored at the time, but stated what he intended to do if he won power—for instance, creating a large army and wiping out the Jews.

The Nazi Party

Set up in 1920 and led by Hitler, the National Socialist German Worker's (Nazi) Party believed blond, white Germans were a master race.

Nazi rallies

The Nazis regularly held vast rallies, where members paraded with banners and listened to speeches from Hitler and other leading Nazis. When the Nazi Party came to power in Germany in 1933, it held a rally every year in Nuremberg, south Germany, showing its strength, determination, and Hitler's power over his party.

Nazis at the
Nuremberg Rally
of 1935

Heading to war

In 1933, Hitler's Nazi Party came to power in Germany and began to build its army. In 1936, Hitler sent troops to the Rhineland—a German industrial area next to France and Belgium—then took over Austria and parts of Czechoslovakia. Meanwhile, Italy invaded parts of the Mediterranean and North Africa, and Japan invaded China. Strong ties grew between Germany, Italy, and Japan. By the late 1930s, Britain and France were re-equipping their armies, while the US watched Japan's rise with concern. The world was preparing for war.

Treaty of Versailles
After its defeat in World War I, Germany was forced to sign a treaty in 1919. It lost its empire and was banned from having a large army. Most Germans supported Hitler's refusal to accept these terms.

Events in North Africa
Italy's leader, Mussolini, wanted to build a new Roman Empire in North Africa and turn the Mediterranean into an "Italian lake." Italy invaded Abyssinia (now Ethiopia) in 1935, sending Emperor Haile Selassie, right, into exile.

Japan invades China
After taking over the Chinese province of Manchuria in 1932, Japan launched a full-scale invasion of China in 1937, seizing the capital, Nanking, and much of the coast.

Hitler moves into Austria

In March 1938, Hitler took his troops into Austria and declared an *Anschluss* (union) between the countries, breaking the Treaty of Versailles. Most Austrians favored the union, but nearby countries were concerned at Hitler's growing power.

Dictators unite

Italy's leader, Mussolini (left), was at first hostile to Hitler (right) because Hitler wanted to invade Austria, Italy's neighbor. Gradually, the countries drew closer and formed a partnership in 1936, the Rome–Berlin Axis, which later included Japan. In 1939, Germany and Italy signed a formal alliance, the Pact of Steel, and fought together early in the war.

Britain and France together

This 1938 visit of King George VI (far left) and Queen Elizabeth to France marked Britain and France's close ties. They were alarmed by Germany and Italy's growing strength and, in 1939, agreed to help Poland, Romania, and Greece if Germany or Italy attacked.

A peaceful approach

In 1938, European leaders agreed to placate Hitler and signed the Munich Agreement. This let Germans in the Sudeten area of Czechoslovakia unite with Germany. British Prime Minister Neville Chamberlain (above) said it guaranteed peace. Six months later, Hitler took over all Czechoslovakia.

Invasion of Poland

Hitler demanded the Polish Corridor—a strip of Poland dividing East Prussia from the rest of Germany. Poland resisted, so he took it; German forces here are seen dismantling the border posts in 1939. In response, Britain and France declared war on Germany— World War II had begun.

Preparing for the worst

Portable warning
Loud, wooden rattles were issued to patrol members of the British Air Raid Precautions (ARP), used to warn of potential gas attacks.

War loomed 1938–39, so Britain, France, Italy, and Germany prepared for the worst, with plans to ration food and raw materials. France had already built the Maginot Line to defend it from German invasion. Britain expected its major cities to be bombed soon, so took care to protect its people, digging shelters, issuing gas masks, and evacuating city children to the countryside. War broke out in September 1939, but it was the German invasions of April–May 1940 that really tested these precautions.

Guarding the Home Front
At the end of the war, all German men ages 16–60 not already in the army were called to the Volkssturm (home guard). They had little training and had to make do with what weapons they could find.

Troops and weapons are transported on the Maginot underground railroad

French defense
The Maginot Line, France's main fortification, took five years to construct (1929–34) and stretched along France's eastern border with Germany. It consisted of antitank defenses, bomb-proof artillery shelters, and forts, many linked by underground rail lines.

Tin-can mortar bomb

Grenade made from a wine bottle

Improvising
The British Home Guard had few weapons and so improvised, using cans to make mortar bombs and bottles for grenades. This volunteer unit protected defense installations and watched out for enemy infiltration.

German gas mask

Gas masks
Everyone in Britain was issued a gas mask. In Germany, only those considered high risk, such as children, air-raid wardens, and Nazi Party officials, were given masks. Gas was never used by either side, so the masks were never needed.

Gas filter

S.Filtereinsatz für den zivilen Luftsch...
...et gegen alle chemischen Kampfstoffe sowie gegen saure Ga...
...gegen Schwebstoffe (Nebel und Rauche) Schützt nicht geg...

"The enemy sees your light! Make it dark!"

This German poster warns civilians to keep all lights shielded at night or risk helping enemy bombers to find their town. Blackouts were compulsory throughout Germany and Britain.

Balloon protection

Large barrage balloons protected Britain's cities from air raids. They were launched before a raid and trailed steel cables beneath them. Bombers had to fly high to avoid the cables, reducing their accuracy.

Air-raid shelters

Most British city-dwellers installed underground Anderson shelters (corrugated-iron tunnel) in their yards. In February 1941, Morrison shelters (steel cages for use indoors) were available for those without yards.

German civilian ration card

German rationing

Food and gasoline were rationed from the outset. Subsidized food offered a healthier diet for the poor than before the war. But in 1943, rationing became severe.

Beach defense

Mines were planted to defend possible invasion beaches in southern Britain and northern France.

British beach mine

Lightning

"Blitzkrieg" (German for "lightning war") was a fast and ferocious military attack used by Germany in which highly mobile Panzer (armored) forces blasted into enemy territory. When Poland was attacked, in September 1939, Britain and France declared war on Germany. From May to June 1940, Germany overpowered France and the Low Countries, despite having fewer tanks and troops than the combined forces of Britain, France, and Belgium. But Germany did have air superiority, and triumphed by June 1940.

German foreign minister Joachim von Ribbentrop

Soviet foreign minister Vyacheslav Molotov

Soviet leader Josef Stalin

Nazi-Soviet pact
On August 23, 1939, the Soviets and German foreign ministers signed a nonaggression pact so Germany could invade Poland and western Europe. They met again (left) to confirm the division of Poland between them.

Dropping bomb

British newspaper announces the start of the war

War declared
Britain and France declared war against Germany on September 3, 1939. But most European countries, including Switzerland and Spain, together with the US, remained neutral.

Motorcycle advance
German Panzer units used motorcycles with sidecars to drive fast into enemy land ahead of the main army, surprising the enemy.

Panzer attack
Tanks were the main power behind the Blitzkrieg (portrayed here in a movie), supported by air bombers. They were so fast in crushing enemy positions they often had to wait for the infantry to catch up.

Dive-bombers

The Junkers Ju87 (Stuka) dive-bomber was the main attacking aircraft in the Blitzkrieg. The bombers were equipped with screaming sirens as they dived to drop their bombs.

Throwing bombs

Grenades were used by the German infantry as they advanced into enemy territory, to kill enemy troops and clear buildings of snipers.

Hand grenade

Stick grenade

Taking France

This photograph of Calais shows the devastation after a Blitzkrieg bombing raid. Such rapid destruction led to France's collapse within six weeks.

Taking the Low Countries

In May 1940, heavily armed German troops poured into Belgium, Luxembourg, and the Netherlands. Their forces were no match for the German army and they soon surrendered.

Stick grenade is tucked into boot so it can be drawn quickly

Occupation

People reacted differently to German occupation. Some joined the resistance (to undermine German plans) or refused to cooperate; others supported the Germans' anti-Communist and anti-Jewish policies. But for most, there was little choice but to accept. France and Norway's governments collaborated with Germany. The leaders of Poland, Czechoslovakia, Norway, the Netherlands, Greece, Luxembourg, and Yugoslavia fled to London, where they set up governments in exile. The kings of Belgium and Denmark stayed, the former as a prisoner. The real power always lay with the occupying Germans.

Plaque of the LVF

Ear piece

Hitler visits Paris nine days after the Nazis took control

Brothers in arms
The French Légion de Volontaires Français (LVF) was anti-Communist and raised volunteers to fight with the Germans against the USSR.

Hitler in Paris
German troops entered an undefended Paris on June 14, 1940. Two million citizens fled, but Parisian life continued much as before, with German officers mixing with locals.

Homemade wireless receiver used by a Dutch family during the occupation

A French collaborator has her hair cropped

Secret radio
Radios were forbidden in many occupied countries, so people made their own secret radios, such as this one used by a Dutch family to listen to Britain's BBC. Broadcasts included war news, messages from exiled royals, and coded messages to secret agents.

The collaborators
Throughout occupied Europe, many people collaborated with the Germans. As countries were liberated, some locals took revenge against the collaborators by beating or shooting them, or by shaving the women's heads.

Operation Dynamo

Between May 26 and June 4, 1940, 338,226 soldiers were evacuated from the French beaches of Dunkirk. The German army sped through France toward the English Channel, trapping the British and French armies. Ships sailed back and forth to rescue the soldiers. The battle of France was a huge defeat for the British army, but the successful evacuation raised morale.

Lapel badge bearing the Vichy State double-headed ax

English Cross of St. George

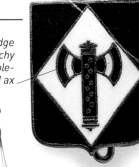

New Symbols

During Vichy rule, many symbols of Republican France were replaced by Vichy symbols, such as the double-headed ax and portraits of Marshal Pétain.

REVOLUTION NATIONALE

Vichy France

On June 12, 1940, French leader Marshal Pétain agreed to German occupation in the north and west while he headed a puppet state, which was really controlled by Germany, from Vichy. His government collaborated with the Germans, but in November 1942, the Germans took over and the state collapsed in August 1944.

To the rescue

At only 14 ft (4.4 m) long, *Tamzine* was the smallest of 900 boats in Operation Dynamo. Others ranged from minesweepers and destroyers to pleasure craft and fishing boats. *Tamzine* ferried many men from the beach to the deep-water vessels.

Tamzine, the smallest civilian vessel to cross the Channel during Operation Dynamo

TAMZINE

Showing support
Resistance groups often wore armbands, like this one from the Polish Home Army, which led the Warsaw Uprising in August 1944, but was crushed.

The color of freedom
Dutch resistance groups were very effective, providing support and shelter for Jews and assisting Allied airborne troops.

Resistance

At first, armed resistance was scattered, with heroic individuals helping Allied servicemen or Jews. Gradually, arms and intelligence from Britain supported organized groups, while Communist groups in Eastern Europe received help from the USSR after 1941. As the Germans became harsher, using slave labor and rounding up peoples they deemed "subhuman," resistance increased. When liberation came (1944–45), partisan groups were fighting with the British, US, and Soviet forces.

King Christian X
When Germany invaded Denmark on April 9, 1940, King Christian X stayed, unlike other countries' monarchs. His government avoided cooperating with Germany and helped Jews escape.

Free French forces
When France fell, General Charles de Gaulle fled to London and broadcast an appeal for people to fight for Free France.

Genuine stamp

Fake stamp

Spot the difference
Communicating by mail was risky. The Germans intercepted letters from the French Resistance, leading to the death of members. To make sure they knew which letters to trust, the British printed French stamps and changed one tiny detail.

French ID

Fake stamps show a larger bag under the left eye

Danish spies
As conditions under the Germans worsened, a large Danish resistance spied for Britain and carried out strikes.

Yeo-Thomas's fake identity card as François Tirelli

Secret lives
Forged documents gave undercover agents new identities. British agent Forest Frederick Edward Yeo-Thomas worked with the French Resistance on three missions. He was caught in 1944 and tortured by the Gestapo, but survived.

Skeleton butt—a lightweight frame

Resistance-made guns
This 9-mm Mark II submachine gun was built by the Danish resistance, based on the British Sten, which was light, simple to use, and easy and cheap to make.

Trigger

Attacking from the bushes
French resistance began as soon as the German armies entered France in May 1940. By 1941, there were a few organized, more effective, armed resistance groups (left), known as the Maquis (meaning bush or scrub) because they hid in the undergrowth then sprung out to fight.

Up the sleeves
The Free French forces used knives hidden in their lapels or up their sleeves to escape their captors. Their badge—the Cross of Lorraine—is on the knife's sheath.

A sheath is attached to an armband worn under clothes

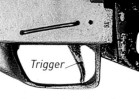

Brave widow
Violette Szabo joined the Special Operations Executive (SOE) after her husband died fighting for the Free French army. She was twice dropped into France, but was captured and died in a concentration camp.

Silencer eliminates most of the sound of the blast

P.BERETTA-CAL. 9 SCURT - M° 1934 - BREVET.
GARDONE V.T-1941

Silent weapons
This silenced 9-mm Beretta pistol was used by the Organizzazione di Vigilanza e Repressione dell'Antifascismo (OVRA), set up to suppress resistance to Italian Fascism.

Tito's Partisans
The most successful European resistance group, the Yugoslav Partisans (left), was organized by Communist Party leader Tito, with 150,000 members. In 1944, combined Partisan and Soviet Red Army forces regained Yugoslavia from the Germans.

German army

The German armed services were a tangle of different organizations, each reporting to Hitler as Commander-in-Chief. These included the Wehrmacht (the regular army), the Schutzstaffel (SS)—originally Hitler's bodyguard, with many secret police (Gestapo) in the ranks—and the armed Panzer (tank) divisions, the navy (Kriegsmarine), the air force (Luftwaffe), reserve forces, militias, and Brownshirts. Uniforms and emblems gave a strong identity and attracted a young, loyal force.

Death's head emblem

Field cap

Divisional badge

Collar patch with the insignia of the SS

Dressed to kill
SS Panzer troops wore black, tight, short jackets (*panzerjacke*) suited for inside the cramped tanks. Their field caps bore the national emblem and the SS death's head.

SS Panzer jacket

Division title "Adolf Hitler"

Belt

SS motto "Meine Ehre heisst Treue" (Loyalty is my honor)

Pants

Heavy armor
Tank troops belonged to the Panzer (German for armor) army. The PzKpfw IV (right) was one of 2,500 tanks that rolled into France in 1940.

Belt webbing

Worn with pride
This national emblem badge was worn by the Waffen-SS—the combat divisions of the SS. At its peak in 1942–43, it had 39 divisions with more than 900,000 soldiers.

Eagle

Swastika—an ancient symbol for good luck

National emblem

Edging

Ankle slit

Loops to tow gun

Hidden horrors
The German's antitank Pak 38 (left) was the only gun able to tackle the well-armored Soviet T34 tanks. It had a range of 9,023 ft (2,750 m) and its low silhouette could be hidden.

Boots

Solid, low-maintenance wheels

General officer's cap

Rank badge for Major General

Oak and laurel leaves

Gold oak-leaf collar patch for general officer

National emblem

Division "Grossdeutschland" (Greater Germany)

Field service tunic

Serving in style

Hitler's new national emblem—a swastika clutched by an eagle—was added to all army uniforms. He kept much traditional army insignia, such as badges for rank. Colored piping showed army branches, such as white for infantry.

Ribbon bar

Iron cross 1st Class, 1939

Hook for dagger

Six barrels were fired consecutively, one second apart

Moaning Minnie

The nebelwerfer (fog thrower, nicknamed "Moaning Minnie" due to the noise it made) fired 70-lb (32-kg) rockets up to 22,639 ft (6,900 m), but each rocket gave itself away with a 40-ft (12-m) bright flame.

Belt with holster

Holster

General officer's breeches

Fob watch pocket

Broad red stripes indicate the wearer was a general officer

Calf laces tighten the bottom of the breeches

General officer's boots

Brownshirts

Sturmabteilung (SA) soldiers were called Brownshirts because of their uniforms. Formed in 1921 to protect Nazi speakers, the force grew to more than 500,000, but was reduced in June 1934 after a power struggle with the army.

SS armband

This armband was worn by Schutzstaffel (SS) members, the most feared Nazi organization. Renowned for violence, the SS also ran concentration camps.

Looking the part

The SS (above) was at first Hitler's personal bodyguard. Its head, Heinrich Himmler, made it a separate security force, with gray coats and death's head cap badges. It was responsible for the worst Nazi crimes.

On the battle line

More than 12.5 million infantry (foot soldiers, like the man above) played a major role in the German army, fighting all the way to the outskirts of Moscow before retreating to defend Berlin.

The Battle of Britain

With the fall of France in June 1940, Hitler hoped Britain might settle for peace. But Britain's new leader, Winston Churchill, had no such intention. So Hitler launched a seaborne invasion—Operation Sea Lion. For this to work, the German air force (Luftwaffe) had to defeat the British Royal Air Force (RAF). From July to October 1940, battles raged across the sky above southeast England, and the RAF slowly won control.

Eight Browning machine guns in edges of wings

Spitfire
The RAF's Spitfire Mk 1A could fly at speeds up to 362 mph (582 kph). It was faster at high altitudes and more maneuverable than the German Messerschmitt Bf109E.

International air force
The RAF had pilots from all around the world who had fled their German-occupied countries. New pilots received a maximum of only 10 hours' training before being sent up to fight.

Two RAF navigators (left) study a map with their Polish pilots

Mobile antiaircraft radar receiver

Detection
RAF radar systems used 300-ft (90-m) steel masts to emit radio signals. The signals bounced off enemy planes and were picked up by radar receivers, alerting pilots to resume battle in the air.

Dogfights
As the RAF and the Luftwaffe fought for control of the skies, dogfights (close battles between fighter aircraft) were common, as portrayed here in the film *Battle of Britain*.

> *"Never in the field of human conflict was so much owed by so many to so few."*
>
> *WINSTON CHURCHILL*

Bf110C Messerschmitts

Messerschmitts

Two types of Messerschmitts formed the fighter mainstay of the Luftwaffe. The Bf110C, an escort fighter for long-range bombers was slow, hard to handle, and inferior to the British Hurricanes and Spitfires. The Bf109E was faster, but its 410-mile (660-km) range limited its effect.

Twin fins on tail

Göring's air force

Luftwaffe Chief, Reichsmarschall Hermann Göring, watched the Battle of Britain from the French coast. He believed they could destroy air defenses in southern England in four days and the RAF in four weeks. But the Luftwaffe failed.

On watch

Ground crews had powerful and sturdy binoculars, such as these used by the Luftwaffe, to watch for enemy aircraft. Both sides radar for long-distance observations. In the air, combat pilots had to stay alert for enemy aircraft.

Direction finder

Powerful lenses

Luftwaffe observation binoculars

Eyepiece

Binoculars rotate for an all-around view of the skies

British fire
service badge

V-2 rocket

Bombing raids

The terrifying drone of enemy bomber planes heralded mass destruction. Each side believed that bombing strategic targets, such as factories, railroads, and oil refineries, would cripple the enemy war effort. Thus, Britain endured the Blitz from 1940–1941, while Germany was bombed repeatedly from 1942 and Japan from 1944.

Two Blitz survivors peer out from the shelter that saved them

Air-raid survival

During air raids, people hid in underground shelters, in cellars, or in makeshift shelters in their own homes. Despite heavy bombing of cities, many people survived.

Bomb power

Late in the war, Germany launched its most secret and deadly weapons. These were the V-1 flying bomb and the V-2 rocket ("V" stood for vengeance). Both bombs carried warheads that weighed almost one ton. They were capable of great damage.

V-2 was 46 ft (14 m) long, weighed 28,660 lb (13,000 kg), and flew at an altitude of 50 miles (80 km)

Firefighting

Most bomb damage was caused by the fires they ignited. Firefighters risked their lives to keep the flames under control, and to save anyone trapped in the burning buildings.

London firemen tackle a blaze in a warehouse, 1941

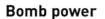

Magnesium incendiary bomb

Incendiary bombs

Thousands of these bombs were dropped on British and German cities; combustible chemicals created immense heat to set buildings alight.

The Blitz

Germany tried to force Britain to surrender during September 1940–May 1941 by bombing its major cities, including London, Liverpool, Glasgow, and Belfast. More than 60,000 civilians were killed and two million homes destroyed in "the Blitz."

Bombers

With bomb loads up to 12,800 lb (5,800 kg), heavy bombers like these US Flying Fortresses could do immense damage.

Bombing of Dresden

The Allied bombing of the German city of Dresden in February 1945 created a firestorm, destroying the city and killing 30,000–60,000 civilians. With few military targets, many condemned the raid as a war crime.

Defend the pilot

Gunners on bomber planes sat or stood in exposed gun turrets to give them a clear view of the skies, and any enemy aircraft.

Dresden still in ruins two years after the raid

Gun sight

German gunner award

The Luftwaffe awarded its war service badge to gunners on a points system; shooting down one enemy aircraft was 4 points; 16 points achieved the award.

Bomber machine gun

Gunners with powerful machine guns were the slow-flying, heavily laden bombers' only defense. When possible, the bombers flew in large convoys escorted by fast, nimble fighter planes to fend off any attack.

Rear machine gun from a Heinkel bomber

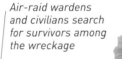

Air-raid wardens and civilians search for survivors among the wreckage

A London street after a night of bombing during the Blitz

Total war

Stalin's shoulder strap

Until mid-1941, the war was fought mainly in Europe and North Africa, between the Axis (Germany, Italy, and some east European countries) and the Allies (Britain, France, and their empires). After France fell, Britain stood alone, but then Germany invaded the USSR, and Japan attacked the US at Pearl Harbor and the British in Malaya. The war was then fought worldwide.

Map showing the extent of Axis control in Europe in 1942

Occupied Europe
By 1942, Germany and Italy occupied most of Europe. The Allies occupied Morocco and Algeria, and drove the Germans from Egypt to Libya.

- Axis states
- Areas controlled by Axis
- Allied states
- Areas controlled by Allies
- Neutral states
- -- Extent of German military occupation

Fighting for France
When Germany invaded France, General Charles de Gaulle (left) went to Britain and raised the banner of Free France, leading overseas French troops and resistance fighters.

German Panzer units pass through a blazing Russian village, torched by fleeing civilians

Into USSR
On June 22, 1941, the Germans attacked the Soviets in Operation Barbarossa. This broke the 1939 Nazi-Soviet Pact and brought the USSR into the war on the side of Britain.

British Prime Minister Winston Churchill (1874–1965)

US President Franklin Roosevelt (1882–1945)

Soviet leader Josef Stalin (1879–1953)

The big three
The leaders of Britain, the USSR, and the US met twice during the war (seen here in February 1945) to coordinate their war efforts.

Pearl Harbor attack
On December 7, 1941, Japan attacked the US naval base of Pearl Harbor in Hawaii, destroying 19 ships and killing 2,403 sailors. On December 8, Congress declared war on Japan and Germany.

Mussolini's Italy

Mussolini (right) and Italy did not join Germany's side until June 1940, when Italy declared war on Britain and France. Italian troops fought with the Germans in the USSR, but Italy remained the junior partner in the Axis.

Hitler and Mussolini drive through Florence, Italy

General Hideki Tojo

Tojo led Japan's pro-military party and became prime minister in October 1941. He sided with Germany and Italy, had Japan attack US and British territory in Asia, and extended Japan's empire. He was tried for war crimes in 1948 and executed.

General Hideki Tojo on the cover of a magazine

Japanese control

By 1942, Japan controlled Southeast Asia and much of the Pacific. In June 1942, the US halted the Japanese advance at Midway.

Japanese-controlled area by 1942

Extent of Japanese expansion

Pearl Harbor under attack

A naval ship explodes during the Japanese bombing

In enemy territory

Many individuals risked their lives by entering enemy-occupied countries to spy, work with resistance fighters, and sabotage enemy plans. The British set up the Special Operations Executive (SOE) and the Americans formed the Office of Strategic Services (OSS) to train spies and devise ways to hide equipment for a mission. Many spies were killed, or captured, tortured, and sent to concentration camps.

Suicide pill
British spies carried an L-pill ("L" stands for lethal), to be swallowed if the spy was captured by the enemy. The pill killed in five seconds. Agents concealed the pills in a variety of ways, such as in lockets, rings, and other jewelry.

Tiny compass   *Concealed compartment*

Plans in the pipe-liner
This pipe was lined with asbestos so that it could be smoked without setting light to the message concealed within it. It also hid a tiny compass.

Blade   *Holes cut for display*

Hidden knife
MI9, a British organization that helped prisoners of war escape, designed this pencil to hide a blade, since a pencil would not arouse suspicion in a search.

End unscrewed to load

Cartridge

Secret agent Sorge
Richard Sorge (above, on a Soviet stamp) was a German journalist spying for the USSR. He learned that Japan was to attack Asia, not the USSR, in 1941, which freed up Soviet troops to fight Germany.

Propelling pencil pistol
By inserting a 6.35-mm cartridge, this pencil became a pistol. The casing contained a spring-loaded hammer to fire the cartridge, released by a button on the side.

Button pulled back to fire

Dangerous date
The SOE sent Odette Sansom to link up with a French Resistance unit, led by Peter Churchill. Both were captured, but they survived and married after the war.

Poison pen threat
Made by the British, this pen fired a gramophone needle when the cap was pulled back and released. It was not lethal—the idea was that users would spread a rumor that the needles were poisoned.

Tuning dial

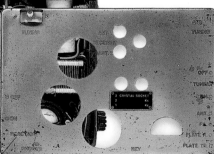

Straps fastened the rubber sole over agent's boots

Cover with English labels

Footprint disguise
The SOE's feet-shaped rubber soles attached to boots for use on a beach to fool the Japanese into thinking they were locals' footprints.

Pocket radio
Abwehr (German military intelligence) issued agents with this small radio to transmit Morse code. All labels were in English so as not to betray the user.

Secrets underfoot

Compartments inside rubber boot heels made ideal hiding places for papers. Both sides used this trick, but heels were often the first place searched when a spy was captured.

Message hidden in the heel

Parachute to death

Not every SOE operation was a great success. Madeleine Damerment parachuted into occupied France in February 1944. She was captured on landing and sent to Dachau concentration camp, where she was executed.

Card tricks

An escape map, divided into numbered sections, was hidden inside playing cards. Escapees would soak the tops and put the sections in order to plot their route home.

Top of card peeled off to reveal map

A foreign match

This matchbox looks French but was made in Britain for SOE agents. Spies abroad could not take anything that might betray their true identity.

Lens opening

Matchbox camera

The US Kodak company developed this so OSS agents could take pictures secretly. The front label was changed according to the country they were in.

Messages from a suitcase

Suitcase radios were used by both sides to broadcast messages from inside enemy territory. Messages were transmitted in Morse code, using a system of sounds in place of letters.

Headphones allowed agents to listen to incoming messages

Plug connected transmitter to power outlet

Frequency dial

Spare valve

Key used to tap out Morse code

Crystal plug used to change transmission frequency

This Mark II radio was used by Oluf Reed Olsen, an agent working for Britain

Battery clips connected transmitter to car battery for power

The prisoners

Many millions of soldiers were captured or surrendered to enemy forces. Most prisoners of war (POWs) spent months or years locked up in specially built prisons. International agreements, such as the Geneva Convention of 1929, were meant to guarantee that prisoners were looked after, but some captors disregarded the agreements. Many prisoners devised ways to escape, but few succeeded. Punishment was severe for those caught.

Marked men
All POWs had to carry identification (ID) tags with them at all times. These two came from the Oflag XVIIA and Stalag VI/A camps in Germany.

Camp currency
Allied POWs in German camps were paid with special camp money (*Lagergeld*) for their work. The money, such as these Reichsmark notes, could buy toothpaste, soap, and sometimes extra food rations.

Polish POWs cook smuggled food on homemade stoves inside their huts at a German prison camp

Buckle blade
Some prisoners snuck in tools. A blade hidden on a belt could cut a prisoner free if he was tied up.

Miniature saw blade

Life in captivity
The Geneva Convention stated that POWs must be clothed, given food and housing as good as their guards, allowed to keep possessions, practice their religion, and receive medical treatment. It was not always kept.

Button compass
A tiny compass could be hidden in a button and used to navigate to safety.

Compass needle

Pivoting blades

Flying away
The building of this glider in Colditz Castle, Germany, was one of many escape plans from this high-security camp. Of the 1,500 POWs there, 176 attempted to escape, but only 31 succeeded.

Clever gadgets
Escape blades were nailed to soldiers' metal shoe heels, or fixed onto coin sides—it was assumed POWs would be able to keep coins.

Nail securing blade to heel

Escape boot
British RAF pilots wore boots that could be cut into civilian shoes with a hidden penknife so the pilots could blend in when in enemy territory and avoid capture.

Men with a mission
The tools (left), made from bedposts and scraps of metal, were used in Colditz to build the escape glider (above).

Homemade plane and saw

Flying boot

Cut-down shoe

KRIEGSGEFANGENENPOST

FOOD	PACKETS
LEBENSMITTEL	PÄCKCHEN
SOAP	1 PIECE
SEIFE	1 STÜCK

PRISONERS' PARCELS
BRITISH RED CROSS & ORDER OF ST. JOHN
WAR ORGANISATION
KRIEGSGEFANGENENPOST

COMITÉ INTERNATIONAL CROIX ROUGE,
GENÈVE—TRANSIT,
SUISSE

Red Cross food package

A rare treat

Under the Geneva Convention, POWs could receive letters and gifts from home. The International Red Cross in Geneva, Switzerland, organized the deliveries. They kept prisoners in touch with home and provided small treats.

Food packages contained luxuries not available in camp

Long journeys

POWs, like these Germans, often traveled hundreds of miles to reach a camp. Italians captured in North Africa were taken to Australia, South Africa, and India; 50,000 other Italians went to the US.

Living with the enemy

After the war, not all prisoners were returned home immediately, and some befriended the locals. Ludwig Maier (second right), a German architect imprisoned in Scotland, wed Englishwoman Lucy Tupper in 1947.

Happy to be alive

In April 1945, 9,000 Soviet POWs were freed by the US from the German Stalag 326 camp (below). Soviet POWs were treated appallingly by the Germans, made to walk for weeks to camps and given starvation rations.

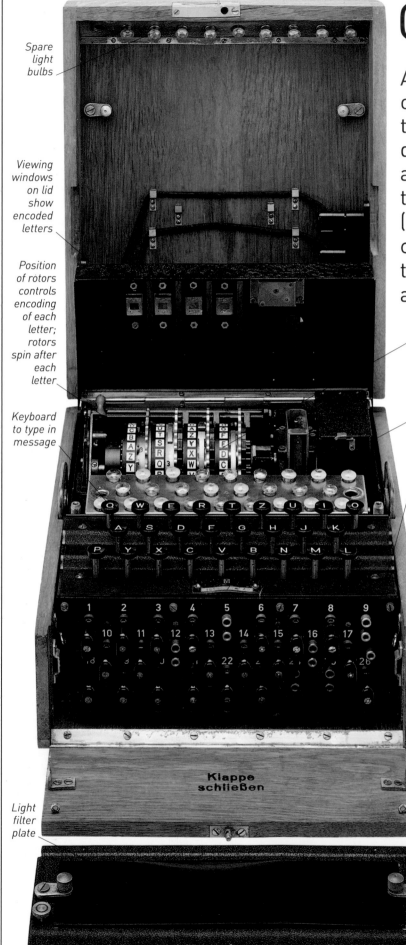

Spare light bulbs

Viewing windows on lid show encoded letters

Position of rotors controls encoding of each letter; rotors spin after each letter

Keyboard to type in message

Light filter plate

Rotor cylinder carries three (later four) alphabetical rotors

Alphabetical lightboard shows final encoded letter

Plugboard settings are changed daily

Klappe schließen

Code-breakers

A code replaces words with letters or symbols. A cipher is a form of code that adds or substitutes letters to disguise it. Both sides used codes and ciphers for messages during the war. Some Allied cryptographers (code-breakers) cracked the Axis codes, revealing valuable information that gave the Allies considerable advantage over their enemies.

Alan Turing
Mathematician Alan Turing was one of the brilliant people working for British Intelligence during the war. He played a key role in deciphering the German Enigma.

Early computers
Scientists and cryptographers at Bletchley Park (the British code-breaking center) developed the "bombe" to decipher German Enigma messages. As Enigma grew more complex, they built Colossus, a forerunner of modern electronic computers.

The German Enigma cipher
The Enigma was the main cipher machine in use during World War II. It enciphered each letter with alphabetical rotors, placed on a cylinder in a predetermined order, and a set of plugs in a plugboard. The settings varied each day, creating millions of possible combinations.

An inside ring

Everyday objects were used to hide microdots—tiny photographs of a coded message that could be read only with a magnifying viewer.

Secret chamber

Screw top

Boris Hagelin

The converted

In the 1930s, Swedish cryptographer Boris Hagelin invented the Converter M-209. It was the main cipher machine used by the US Army during the war.

Fact to fiction

Some code-breakers and spies turned their experiences into fiction, such as Ian Fleming, who worked for British Naval Intelligence.

Ian Fleming, creator of the fictional spy James Bond

Reading aperture

Top cover in open position

Switching unit

Compartment for stepping switches

Stepping switch

Purple cipher

The Japanese Purple machine used a plugboard and telephone switches to create a complex cipher device. US Intelligence cracked Purple's code in September 1940 and built a replica.

Pearl Harbor following the Japanese attack

Concentric disks

Kryha cipher

The Kryha, invented in 1924, used a spring-driven alphabetic rotor to substitute each letter with a different one every time the letter was used in a word. The Germans used the Kryha in the war, not realizing that the US had already broken its code.

Spring motor

Indicating disks

Ignored information

Communications from the Japanese Purple machine detailing an attack on the US in late 1941 were decoded by the US, but the Pearl Harbor target was not clear until it was too late. Code-breaking in 1942 enabled the US to defeat the Japanese navy at Midway.

Pocket-sized novel for US troops

America at war

After the shock of Pearl Harbor, the US transformed its economy into a giant war machine, mass-producing every weapon to win on land, sea, and air. Expenditure on war production rose massively, unemployment disappeared, and wages doubled. Unlike every other country at war, the US boomed and most people had more money to spend than ever before.

Mass production
Aircraft factories played a huge role in turning out arms. US factories built 250,000 aircraft, 90,000 tanks, 350 destroyers, and 200 submarines. By 1944, the US produced 40 percent of the world's arms.

Browning machine gun
The 0.5 Browning machine gun was the standard weapon in US bombers. But even flying in close formation with others, the Browning was no match for German fighter planes.

Spring-loaded pilot parachute

Four main parachutes for a gentle descent

Steel parachute cable

15th Air Force

9th Air Force

Fighting with fire
Flame-throwers (such as used by this US marine on Guadalcanal in the Pacific, 1942) were often used to set light to buildings or destroy protective vegetation and flush out the enemy.

US Strategic Air Forces

US Army Air Force (USAAF) badges
The 15th Air Force in southern Italy bombed German-held targets. The 9th supported the Allies in North Africa and Italy. The 8th, 9th, and 15th later merged into the US Strategic Air Forces in Europe.

Crashpan to cushion wheels on landing

The Mustang had a range of 2,080 miles (3,347 km)

Maximum speed was 437 mph (703 kph)

Droppable fuel tank

Long-range fighter
Early versions of the P-51 Mustang were limited in altitude and range, but a better engine, larger fuel tanks, and a cut-down rear fuselage made the fourth version (P-51 D) one of the best fighter planes of the war. It defended bombers over Germany.

North American P-51 D Mustang

Air break
These P-51 Mustang pilots were part of the 15th US Air Force, based in southern Italy.

B-24 liberator
Having flown all the way from southern Italy, this B-24 Liberator (a heavy bomber with a long range) is flying low as it bombs oilfields in southern Romania.

Central support to which parachutes are attached

Machine gun

Bag for empty cartridge cases

Parachute jeep
US Army jeeps could be dropped by parachute. Developed in 1940, the US jeep was one of the best loved (and envied) of all war vehicles. Its four-wheel drive made it versatile in most terrains.

Protective headgear used in turrets and other combat positions where standard helmets were too big

US aircrew M4 helmet

US jeep could carry an 800-lb (360-kg) load and tow an antitank gun at the same time

Flak jacket weighed 20 lb (9 kg)

Supporting cradle

Parachute release stand

Taking the flak
Flak jackets such as this were worn by US aircrew from 1942 to protect them from antiaircraft fire. By 1944, 13,500 were used by the 8th Air Force in Europe.

Women at work

Before World War II, most women worked within the home. With men away fighting, however, almost every task that had previously been restricted to men was now taken over by women. Women also played an important role in resistance forces. The war could not have been waged and won without women's vital contribution. After the war, attitudes toward women in the workplace changed forever.

Nazi mothers
In Germany, mothers were awarded medals for producing target numbers of children. The Nazis idealized German women as mothers of the new "master race."

Silver (2nd class) medal awarded for bearing six to seven children

New recruits
As more men were required for fighting, posters promising glamour attracted more women into the war effort.

A woman assists with aircraft maintenance

Land girls
One of women's major contributions to the war effort was to run the farms and grow much-needed food. In Britain, the Women's Land Army recruited 77,000 members to carry out arduous tasks, such as plowing and harvesting.

Aircraft maintenance
The shortage of male pilots and mechanics meant that many women learned to fly and maintain planes, delivering and servicing them.

Parachute makers
Seamstresses worked long hours to make parachutes. Many thousands of parachutes were required by the armed services, including pilots and airborne troops dropped into battle from the skies.

Night watch

Many women operated the powerful searchlights that tracked enemy bombers for antiaircraft guns to fire on before the bombers dropped their bombs. Women were not allowed to fire the guns, though. Night work could also mean patrolling the streets as an air-raid warden.

Female searchlight operator scours the night sky for bombers

Gas bag

Everyone had to keep their gas masks with them. This handbag has a special compartment for a mask, although most people carried theirs in cardboard boxes, which women often decorated with fabric.

Gas mask chamber

Pans to planes

Because of the scarcity of iron, tin, and aluminum, posters appealed to housewives for unwanted items. Old pots and pans were melted down for planes. Even old wool sweaters were unraveled and knitted into socks and scarves for the troops.

Frying pan made from the wreckage of a German plane

Crashed enemy planes were sometimes recycled into pans and other utensils

Turn this RAW MATERIAL into WAR MATERIAL!

FURTHER INFORMATION CAN BE OBTAINED FROM :-
THE DIRECTOR of PUBLIC CLEANSING,
· CITY of WESTMINSTER ·
31 CHARING CROSS ROAD, W.C.2.
Tele. TEMPLE BAR 0611. Extension 44

Rosie the riveter

In the US, fictional character Rosie the Riveter became a symbol of the new working woman, as women were needed in factories to replace the 16 million US citizens called into the armed services.

"Rosie the Riveter" by Norman Rockwell for the *Saturday Evening Post*, May 1943

Air-raid training

In India, fear of a Japanese invasion led the government to take precautionary steps, training women for air-raid precaution (ARP) duties (above) and as auxiliaries to support troops in the Far East.

A wartime childhood

Children were as affected by the war as the adults. Their homes were bombed or burned, their fathers were called up to fight, and their mothers went to work. For one group of children in particular, the war brought special fear, as the German authorities sought out Jewish children and sent them to die in concentration camps. For all children, the war robbed them of an education and a normal life.

Growing up in Japan

In school, Japanese children were told their country was superior and their duty was to fight for their emperor. They had to attend military drills and work in the student labor force. When Japanese cities were bombed by the US, 450,000 children were evacuated from the cities.

A wartime version of "happy families"

Ⓗ H...
S. Alt... the Groce...

Ⓖ EV...

Ⓣ T...

Ⓑ EVACUEE
Miss Prim
Eddy Earwig

Ⓖ EVACUEE
Polly Puffer

Blitz games

Themed toys and games, such as this evacuation card game, were produced in the war years. Card games were popular past-times during the long hours spent in air-raid shelters.

Head strap

Protective eyepiece

Air filter

"Mickey mouse" gas mask

Novelty

Colorful "Mickey Mouse" gas masks were issued to British toddlers to make them more fun. Children were taught how to put on their masks in a hurry.

All evacuees wore labels indicating their destinations

These children are waiting for transportation to their new homes in the countryside

Evacuees were allowed to take a favorite toy

Evacuees

The war separated many youngsters from their families. During the Blitz, thousands of British children went to live with foster families in the countryside, or even overseas.

Nazi toys

Propaganda infected all aspects of German life. Even toys glorified the "Aryan" (blond-haired, blue-eyed) race as masters of the world, and put down the Jews.

Armed child partisan in Leningrad, the USSR, 1943

For Fatherland

As the German army swept into the USSR in 1941, many children became orphaned and homeless. Some joined the partisan groups fighting the Germans, running messages, fetching supplies, and even taking part in acts of sabotage.

In hiding

For two years, Jewish girl Anne Frank and her family hid from the Nazis in an attic in the Netherlands, where Anne kept a diary, but they were betrayed. Anne died of typhus in Belsen concentration camp in March 1945.

Paper play

In wartime, all materials were needed for making weapons, so children had simple paper or cardboard toys.

Wild animals made of paper

Hitler Youth membership card

Young Nazis

In 1926, the Hitler Youth became the male youth division of the Nazi Party (girls joined the League of German Girls). In 1943, those age 16 were called up to fight. Younger recruits helped on farms or delivered mail.

Forced to follow Hitler

At first, membership of the Hitler Youth was voluntary. But in 1936, it was made compulsory for all children age 10 to 18.

The Pacific

After their surprise attack on Pearl Harbor in December 1941, the Japanese swarmed across Southeast Asia and advanced, island by island, through the Pacific, south toward Australia, and east to the US. Their goal was to form a huge empire with supplies of all raw materials needed to build military power. Japan seemed invincible, but two massive naval battles—in the Coral Sea in May 1942 and at Midway in June 1942—halted their advance.

Japanese prayer flag
Japanese servicemen carried, or wore around their heads, prayer flags into battle, with prayers and blessings written by relatives on the background of the flag of Japan.

Douglas Devastator bombers prepare for action

Aircraft carrier
Douglas Devastator torpedo bombers (left) were old and lumbering planes used by the US on aircraft carriers. They proved no match for the speedy Japanese Mitsubishi A6M Zero fighters, which knocked out all but four of the USS *Enterprise*'s bombers. But overall, the Japanese suffered a defeat at Midway.

The Coral Sea
The Japanese tried to capture island bases to use for air attacks on Australia. But the US halted their advance south in May 1942 in the first naval battle conducted entirely by aircraft taking off from carriers.

A Japanese aircraft floats in tatters in the Coral Sea after being shot down

Struggle for Guadalcanal Island

US aircraft carrier *Hornet* is under fire from Japanese aircraft at the Battle of Santa Cruz in October 1942. This sea battle was one of many fought around Guadalcanal as Japanese and US forces fought for this strategic base. The US took over the island in February 1943, but Japan's ferocious resistance showed how far they would go to defend territory.

Scale showing degrees north or south of equator

Japanese sextants

The Japanese Navy used sextants to navigate the vast Pacific. Its navy was the third largest in the world (after the US and Britain), with 10 aircraft carriers, 12 battleships, 36 cruisers, 100 destroyers, and a mighty naval air force.

Suicide missions

The battle for the Philippines raged in October 1944 and the desperate Japanese introduced a terrifying weapon: volunteer bomber pilots (Kamikazes) flew planes loaded with explosives onto the decks of US warships to blow them up.

Adjustable eyepiece

Japanese naval sextant for calculating latitude (distance north or south)

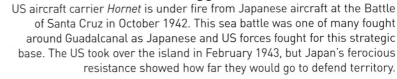

Horizon mirror

Kamikaze pilot ties a hachimaki around his head

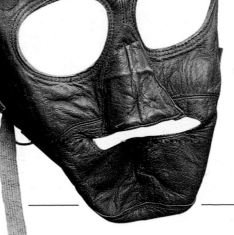

Masked

Japanese pilots wore protective leather masks, which made them look as fierce as their reputation. Most would kill themselves rather than surrender.

Kamikaze pilot

Japanese pilots volunteered for the Kamikaze, certain-death flights, believing it glorious to die for their emperor, or inspired by Japanese military traditions of self sacrifice. They wore the *hachimaki* (headcloth) of the medieval samurai.

Japan

Naval and military ensign

Throughout the war, the Japanese fought on three fronts: for occupation of China in the north; against US, Australian, and New Zealand forces in the Pacific Ocean; and in the jungles of Burma, where the "forgotten war" continued against the British and the Chindits (a British-Burmese fighting unit), who fought to liberate Burma. Many Japanese fought to the death.

Australian "Austen" submachine gun

Australia
Australian forces were heavily involved in the war against Japan—preventing the Japanese from occupying Papua New Guinea in 1942, and, with the US, liberating New Guinea and other islands—as Japan's expansion in Southeast Asia threatened Australia.

A Japanese soldier holds the Rising Sun flag

24-hour rations
British forces in Southeast Asia and the Pacific were issued with food packs (above). A pack provided one man with enough nourishment for an entire day.

US Army field telephone

Loyal fighters
More than 1,700,000 Japanese soldiers obeyed the Soldier Code of 1942, based on the ancient Bushido (warrior) Code of samurai fighters. The code stated that soldiers be loyal to the emperor, and that it was their duty to die rather than face the shame of capture.

Liberating Burma
The battle for Burma was fought on the road between the Indian cities of Kohima and Imphal. The British used Imphal as their base after the Japanese expelled them from Burma in May 1942. The Japanese invaded India in March 1944. British and Indian troops (right) defeated a force of 80,000 and paved the way for Burma's liberation (achieved May 1945).

Portable communications
Field telephones were used by Allied and Japanese soldiers. The speed of the Japanese advances meant troops needed to inform headquarters of their progress and of the whereabouts of the enemy.

Thailand–Burma railroad

The Japanese used diesel-powered traction cars, which could run on rails or roads, from 1942–43. With them, they built a railroad from Thailand to Burma, intending to use it to move troops and supplies throughout their empire.

Saved from starvation

These Dutch POWs were lucky; a quarter of the 103,000 Australian, US, British, and Dutch soldiers taken captive by the Japanese had died in camps by 1944. Asian prisoners suffered worse—at least 100,000 died building the Thailand-Burma railroad alone.

Bridge attack

Railroad bridges along the 258-mile (415-km) long Thailand-Burma railroad were designed and built by POWs. British planes regularly bombed the bridges, hoping to destroy the railroad and halt the Japanese.

Improvised glasses and comb

Captured

POWs held by the Japanese were given few provisions and had to improvise. The Japanese had no respect for POWs, and worked many of them to death building railroads and roads.

A US memorial of marines hoisting the flag on Mt. Suribachi, Iwo Jima

Raising the flag

In February 1945, US marines stormed Iwo Jima, a tiny island south of Japan. The Japanese defended the island to the bitter end. After suffering losses, the US bombed mainland Japanese cities and later dropped two atomic bombs.

The Battle of the Atlantic

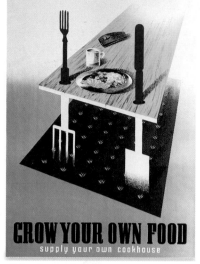

...every available piece of land must be cultivated

GROW YOUR OWN FOOD
supply your own cookhouse

Throughout the war, a battle raged in the North Atlantic Ocean between the Allies and the Germans, as German U-boats (submarines) and destroyers attacked supply ships from the US. The German navy was smaller than the Allies', but its U-boats reigned supreme. However, the Allies' greater use of the convoy system, long-range aircraft patrols, quick-response anti-submarine warships, and improved radar saw the battle turn in the Allies' favor by mid-1943.

Dig for victory

Overseas imports of food were hampered by the war. In Britain, to ensure supplies of fruit and vegetables, a "Dig for Victory" campaign urged people to grow food. Every spare bit of fertile land became a vegetable patch.

Equipped with 88 guns, including 20 long-range and 68 antiaircraft guns

Periscope

Wet-and-dry exit and reentry chamber

Sinking the *Bismarck*

One of the largest (allegedly unsinkable) German battleships, the *Bismarck* set off from Gdynia in the Baltic on May 18, 1941, sailed around Iceland, sank Britain's HMS *Hood*, and was destroyed by a British fleet on May 27.

Main steering wheel

Helmsman's seat

First lieutenant's seat frame

Periscope

German Biber

Armed with two torpedoes, Biber submarines operated off the coast of northern France and the Netherlands from 1944–45, damaging Allied cargo and cross-Channel ships supplying forces in western Europe.

Inside a midget

The British X-craft midget submarine, crewed by four, handled special missions during the Battle of the Atlantic. One submarine disabled the German battleship *Tirpitz*, which threatened British convoys heading to the USSR.

Distilled water tank

Wooden deckboard

Log tank

Cradle for oxygen bottle

Freshwater tank

Viewing port

Towing eye

Warhead

> *"We all snapped our hands to our caps, glanced at the flag, and jumped... In the water we were pushed together in a bunch, as we bobbed up and down like corks."*
>
> LIEUTENANT BURKHARD VON MULLENHEIM-RECHBERG, BISMARCK *SURVIVOR*

Up periscope

Safe beneath the surface, U-boat crews used periscopes to watch Allied convoys and select targets for their torpedoes and guns. But when U-boats were close to the surface, they were easily detectable from the air and Allied planes destroyed many of them.

U-boat officer uses a periscope to locate enemy ships

The ship was 823 ft (251 m) long

Gun is aimed ready to fire at enemy ships and U-boats

Under attack

When underwater, U-boats (above) were vulnerable to depth charges dropped from Allied ships or aircraft; on the surface, to bombs, torpedoes, or shells; and in shallow waters, to mines. Only a quarter of German submarines survived the war.

A sailor on board a warship accompanying an Atlantic convoy keeps a lookout for enemy aircraft

Torpedo

Rudder

Propeller

Atlantic convoy

Single merchant ships crossing the North Atlantic were vulnerable to attack from U-boats and so traveled in large convoys with warships and air cover. Convoys traveled at the speed of their slowest member, making the trip very dangerous. Many sailors died.

Stalingrad

German bronze tank assault badge

Germany invaded the Soviet Union in 1941. The Germans advanced north toward Leningrad, east toward Moscow, and south to the wheat fields and oil wells and to Stalingrad—important as the namesake of Soviet leader Stalin. The battle for Stalingrad saw vast losses on both sides. In early 1943, the destruction of the German army and its surrender marked a turning point in the war—Germany was no longer unbeatable.

In the snow
War in the Soviet Union was aggravated by the freezing winter, for which the Germans were ill-equipped. The Soviets were more used to the weather and had quilted undersuits, white camouflaged oversuits, fur hats, and felt boots.

Red Army weaponry
Thousands of submachine guns, such as this PPS43, were cheaply and quickly made and issued to the Red Army.

Trigger

Hooded foresight

Hand grip

Forward hand grip

Soviet submachine gun

Shoulder butt

Hand grenades
Soviets used these to stop the enemy advance in Stalingrad.

Standard issue
The 0.3-in (7.62-mm) Tokarev TT33 semiautomatic pistol was the standard issue gun given to Soviet officers, airmen, and tank crews.

Battle of Stalingrad
In August 1942, the German 6th Army attacked from the west and pushed the defenders into buildings along the Volga River. The Soviets counterattacked in November, encircling the 6th Army. The Germans were forced to surrender in February 1943.

Shootout
Germans and Soviets fought over every building in Stalingrad. Hand-to-hand fighting was widespread, and anyone showing himself was likely to be killed by sniper fire.

Red Army cavalry

Red Army cavalry could move fast to the front line to support the infantry. Both sides used horses to tow supplies, but horses were easily bogged down by wet mud or snow in winter.

Red Army cavalry brandish swords as they charge through the snow

T-34 was armed with a 3.3-in (85-mm) gun after 1943

The casualties

About 91,000 German soldiers were captured at the end of the battle of Stalingrad, which saw both sides lose about 500,000 soldiers each. Two million Stalingrad civilians lost their lives. Amazingly, 10,000 civilians lived in the city throughout the battle and survived.

German soldiers suffer a harsh Soviet winter

Tank superior

The Soviet T-34 tank, designed in 1939, was the mainstay of the Red Army armored units; 39,698 were built between 1941 and 1945 to carry a crew of five—one commander, two gunners, a loader, and a driver. With a speed of 32 mph (51 kph), the tank could cover 250 miles (400 km) without refueling. The slower German tanks were no match for them.

Gun mounted in swiveling turret

T-34 diesel engine functions well in severe cold

Total weight 71,681 lb (32,514 kg)

Straw boots worn by German sentries in the Soviet Union

Frostbite

German soldiers fashioned snow boots out of straw to try to keep their feet warm and dry, as their stiff leather boots were too tight for layers of socks and too porous to keep out damp. Many suffered frostbite during Soviet winters.

Wide tracks are ideal for crossing soft, uneven terrain

Inside the USSR

The Soviet Union had spent two years getting ready for war, but nothing could have prepared it for the suffering inflicted upon it—20 million Soviets died, with millions enslaved by the Germans or killed in work camps. Yet civilians worked hard for victory and the war became known as the Great Patriotic War.

Resistance fighters
Posters urged Soviets in German-occupied territory to join the partisans living in forests and *"Beat the enemy mercilessly."*

Residents of Leningrad abandon their homes destroyed by Nazi bombs

Red Star   Red Banner

Awards
The main medals awarded to Soviet soldiers were the Hero of the Soviet Union and the Orders of the Red Banner and the Red Star. Stalin also introduced the Orders of Kutuzov and Suvorov.

Water, water everywhere...
During the Soviet winter of 1941, the temperature in Leningrad fell to -40°F (-40°C). Food ran out and water supplies froze. People had to gather snow and ice and thaw it.

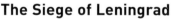

The Siege of Leningrad
The longest siege of the war took place in the Soviet city of Leningrad. German troops, supported by Finns, surrounded the city in September 1941. The Germans dropped more than 100,000 bombs and 200,000 shells and killed 200,000 citizens, but failed to capture the city. The siege was eventually lifted by the Red Army in January 1944.

Feeding the city

During the Leningrad siege, every spare bit of ground was used to grow food, but rationing remained strict. More than 630,000 civilians died from starvation and the extreme cold.

Harvesting vegetables in a cathedral square, Leningrad

Mayakovsky subway station in Moscow being used as an air-raid shelter

Attack on Moscow

Under attack from German troops in October 1941, many civilians sheltered in the subway station. In December, the Soviets counterattacked and the German forces, suffering from low supplies and the harsh winter, pulled back.

1942 poster urges Soviets to *"Follow this worker's example, produce more for the front"*

Produce more!

Despite this strong male image, more than half the Soviet workforce by the end of the war was female, playing a huge role in the defeat of Hitler by producing essential war equipment.

Snipers

Red Army snipers were engaged to shoot the enemy one by one. When a sniper achieved 40 kills, he was called a "noble sniper."

Soviet sniper rifle

Wooden hand-guard

Foresight

The Molotov cocktail

Finnish troops in the Russo-Finnish War used "Molotov cocktail" gas bombs, named after the Soviet politician Vyacheslav Molotov.

The Russo-Finnish war

After Germany invaded Poland in 1939, the Soviet Union tried to secure its western front and invaded Finland. The Finns fought back but, in March 1940, were forced to accept a peace treaty. The Soviets lost thousands more soldiers than the Finns, revealing Red Army weaknesses.

Finnish Lahti 0.8-in (20-mm) L39 anti-tank rifle

Wooden cheek-rest

Rubber recoil pad

Desert fighting

In September 1940, Italy invaded Egypt from its colony of Libya, but the British overwhelmed the Italians. Italy's ally Germany sent troops to North Africa in February 1941, and a two-year desert battle was fought until the British 8th Army beat the German Afrika Korps at El Alamein in November 1942. US and British troops, landing in Morocco and Algeria, advanced east to surround the retreating Germans, forcing the Afrika Korps and their Italian allies to surrender in May 1943.

Sly desert fox
Field Marshal Erwin Rommel (1891–1944), far left, commander of the German Afrika Korps, was known as the Desert Fox. He had the ability to assess a situation quickly and "sniff" out his enemy's weak points.

Battle of Tobruk
The Mediterranean port of Tobruk, eastern Libya, was first held by the Italians, then captured by the British in early 1941, and then by the Germans in June 1942. The British recaptured it after El Alamein in November 1942. Pictured: a scene from the 1967 film *Tobruk*.

British troops advancing in the sand at El Alamein

El Alamein
The German Afrika Korps reached El Alamein by October 1942. This key coastal town was the gateway to Egypt and the Suez Canal (a shipping lane linking the Mediterranean to the Red Sea). Here, they met the British 8th Army and were defeated in a 12-day battle. The British victory marked a turning point in the war.

German antitank mine

British mine detector

Mine alert
Minefields were laid around El Alamein by both sides, causing many deaths as tanks and infantry tried to navigate around them. A vast number still remain buried in the desert.

On the lookout in Libya
The German Afrika Korps, formed in 1941, used "donkey's ears binoculars" to view the enemy. It relied on Mediterranean convoys for reinforcements and supplies, which were attacked by the British.

Invasion of Italy's Sicily
The German defeat in North Africa opened the way for the Allies to invade Europe, but the Allies did not want to risk a direct attack against German forces. Instead, they invaded Italy, hoping to force it out of the war.

Commonwealth help
Some units wore Arab-style cloth headwear suited to the hot African sun. New Zealand units, including a Maori (native New Zealander) battalion, joined the British 8th Army.

Cloth wrap kept out sand and sun

Well led
Field Marshal Montgomery (above) led the British 8th Army. Monty's attention to detail and concern for troop morale contributed to his army's victory at El Alamein.

Inside, a crew of six manned the tank

Camouflaged in desert colors

Monty's tank
Montgomery had his own tank, a US Grant M3A3, used for observation on battlefields, and in the invasion of Sicily and Italy.

Propaganda

The war was fought with propaganda (spreading ideas) as much as ammunition, as both sides needed to convince their people that the war was right and that their side would win. Both sides manipulated public opinion to keep up morale and also used propaganda to break down enemy morale. Some propaganda was crude and some was subtle. Movies, radio, leaflets, and posters were all used in the battle for hearts and minds, while performers traveled to entertain homesick troops.

Hitler the leader
Propaganda did much to boost Hitler's image as a visionary leader, showing him surrounded by adoring followers and depicted as a great statesman who would achieve world domination.

Tokyo Rose
Iva Toguri D'Aquino, known by the sarcastic GI nickname of Tokyo Rose, remains the only US citizen convicted of treason (serving 10 years in prison) and then pardoned. Trapped in Japan after Pearl Harbor, she worked on a Japanese radio show, broadcasting anti-US propaganda.

British airmen load up with propaganda fliers

Bombarding the enemy with ideas
British and US bombers dropped six billion leaflets over occupied Europe. Some warned civilians in occupied countries against cooperating with the enemy. Others told soldiers their efforts were futile and urged them to surrender.

An umbrella caricatures the British soldier

German armband

Japanese insignia

Kick out Brits
Italians wanted the Mediterranean to be an "Italian lake" and were attempting to kick the British out of North Africa. This 1942 Italian cartoon shows the Germans and the Japanese doing the same.

EUROPA

MEDITERRANEO

AFRICA

ASIA

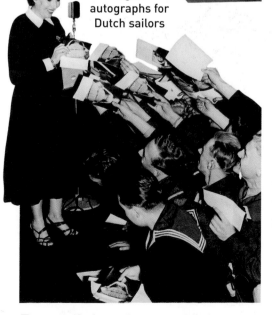

*French
Tricolor*

British Union Jack

Allied power

Simple visual images were effective propaganda. This 1943 US poster shows the four Allied nations pulling apart the Nazi swastika. Constant reminders that the combined strength of the Allied nations would overcome the Axis did much to lift morale.

*US Stars
and Stripes*

*USSR Hammer and
Sickle on Red Flag*

Vera Lynn
signs
autographs for
Dutch sailors

Samurai destroyer

This poster portrays Japan as a samurai warrior and celebrates the Axis's might after Japan sunk two British warships in December 1941.

US war gods

A 1945 Chinese leaflet says this American pilot chased the Japanese out of the Chinese sky but needs help when hurt, lost, or hungry, telling rural Chinese which nations were friendly.

Entertaining the troops

British singer Vera Lynn, the "forces' sweetheart," was one of many entertainers who performed soothing and sentimental songs to keep troops' morale high.

The Holocaust

The Holocaust was the Nazi attempt to exterminate Europe's Jews. The Nazis were anti-Semitic (prejudiced against Jews), and sent Jews to concentration camps where many were worked to death. In the "Final Solution," they set up extermination camps to kill huge numbers of Jews each day. More than six million Jews were murdered.

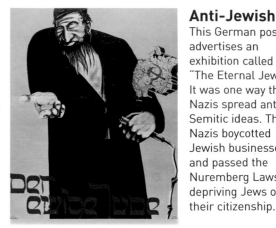

Anti-Jewish
This German poster advertises an exhibition called "The Eternal Jew." It was one way the Nazis spread anti-Semitic ideas. The Nazis boycotted Jewish businesses and passed the Nuremberg Laws, depriving Jews of their citizenship.

First impressions
Many Jews sent by rail to camps thought they were being sent to work in eastern Europe.

Warsaw ghetto
In 1940, Jews in the Polish capital, Warsaw, were herded into a walled ghetto. Conditions inside were awful and many died. In 1943, the Nazis attacked the ghetto to wipe it out. The Jews fought back; only 100 escaped.

Jews are rounded up in the Warsaw ghetto at gunpoint

The yellow star
From 1942, Jews in German-occupied Europe had to wear a yellow star. This made it easy to identify them.

Extermination camps
The Nazis set up concentration camps for Jews, communists, homosexuals, political prisoners, Roma, and other "undesirables." Eight extermination camps, notably Auschwitz (below) in Poland, had gas chambers to speed up the killing of inmates.

Auschwitz concentration camp in Poland is preserved as a permanent reminder of the Holocaust

Crematoria

The bodies of dead inmates were stripped of clothes, hair, jewelry, and gold teeth, and piled up for cremation. The crematoria were run by fellow prisoners, some of whom rebelled in Auschwitz.

A Hungarian Jew, a Belsen survivor

Stretchers were used to place bodies in the furnaces

Feeding bowl

This empty tin can, utilized by an inmate, once contained cyanide gas crystals used in the gas chambers.

Camp conditions

Conditions were appalling. Food was scarce, workers endured 12-hour shifts, and many officers abused inmates. Others conducted horrific experiments on both living and dead prisoners.

Facing the truth

Allied troops marched local Germans into some camps to see the Nazi atrocities. As the camps were liberated by the Allied armies, the Holocaust horror became clear.

SS guards captured at Belsen

Punishing the guards

For the Allied troops liberating the camps, the gruesome reality was too much to bear, and some shot the German SS guards. Some guards were made to bury the dead; others were put on trial for crimes against humanity.

Intelligent postcards
Allied intelligence used postcards of Normandy, plus maps, aerial photographs, and information from spies, to build up a picture of the coastline before invasion.

"Sword," the codename for one landing beach

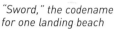

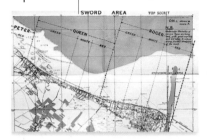

"Sword" beach
This intelligence map details what the soldiers would encounter as they waded ashore. "Sword" (the most eastern beach), "Juno," and "Gold" were stormed by the British and Canadian forces; western "Omaha" and "Utah" by the US.

D-Day invasion

In the early morning of June 6, 1944 (D-Day), Operation Overlord—the Allied invasion of France—took place on Normandy beaches after years of planning. More than 150,000 US, British, and Canadian soldiers were ferried across the English Channel to establish five beachheads (shorelines captured from the enemy). The Germans were expecting an invasion farther to the east and had set up a defense there. By nightfall, the beachheads were secure. The liberation of German-occupied Europe had begun.

Sky attack
Parachutists played an important role on D-Day. In the early hours, US Army paratroopers dropped behind "Utah" beach to secure vital positions. British paratroopers landed behind "Sword" beach and destroyed a German battery (gun site).

"Omaha" invasion
The most difficult landing site was "Omaha" beach, surrounded by high cliffs and with few routes inland. The US troops sustained 3,000 casualties but established a 2-mile (3-km) deep beachhead by nightfall.

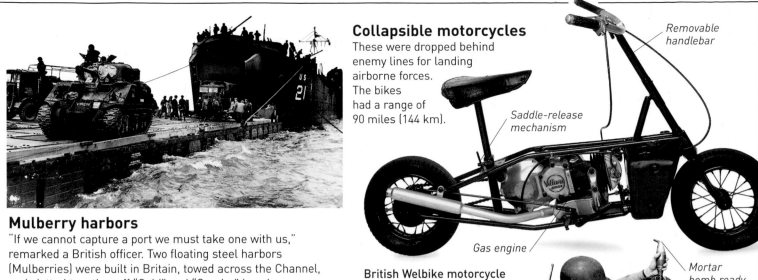

Mulberry harbors

"If we cannot capture a port we must take one with us," remarked a British officer. Two floating steel harbors (Mulberries) were built in Britain, towed across the Channel, and slotted together off "Gold" and "Omaha" beaches.

Collapsible motorcycles

These were dropped behind enemy lines for landing airborne forces. The bikes had a range of 90 miles (144 km).

Removable handlebar

Saddle-release mechanism

Gas engine

British Welbike motorcycle

On the beach

The day after D-Day, trucks, tanks, and troops flooded in to the beaches. The first wave of soldiers made each beach as safe as possible from enemy attack. Then ships unloaded vast amounts of equipment.

Barrage balloons to protect supplies from overhead attacks

Explosive work

The Allies pressed inland, encountering snipers, tanks, and fortifications hidden in the hedgerows. Progress was slow, but they soon had a million men in France.

Mortar bomb ready to fire

Liberation

Liberation from the Axis took a long time. The Red Army slowly pushed the Germans out of the USSR, but fighting continued in the Balkans into 1945. The Allied liberation of Italy from fascist rule was slow; liberation of France began only in June 1944. Denmark, Norway, and parts of Austria and the Netherlands were under Nazi rule until the Germans surrendered in May 1945. The Philippines, most of Burma, and some islands were recaptured from the Japanese by the end of the war.

Soldiers crawl over the rubble of the monastery at Monte Cassino

Liberation of Paris

The Germans occupied Paris from June 14, 1940. In August 1944, the Resistance rose up, Free French forces stormed the city, and the Germans surrendered. Free French leader General de Gaulle led a victory march (right).

Battle for a free Italy

After the Allied liberation of Sicily in July 1943, Italy surrendered, changed sides, and declared war on Germany. German troops entered Italy, forcing the Allies to fight their way up the country, such as in the battle of Monte Cassino (above).

Freed from fascism

In January 1945, Allied forces entered northern Italy, helped by partisans of the Resistance Army, who fought to bring down Mussolini's government, expel the Germans from Italy, and execute Mussolini.

Sandbags to absorb bullets

Italian partisans in the liberation of Milan

Bronze eagle

Hitler's eagle
This bronze eagle once hung in Hitler's official residence in Berlin. Captured by the Soviets during the final battle for Berlin, a Red Army officer gave it to a British soldier in 1946.

Shrapnel ripped a hole through the wing

French freedom
The liberation of France was complete in early 1945. Nazi swastikas were ripped down and replaced with the French tricolor. The Free French, led by General de Gaulle, set up a government to take over from the Germans.

Two women tear down a sign in front of Nazi headquarters in Troyes, France

De-Nazification
With the Germans gone, local people removed all evidence of their former Nazi rulers. German-language signs and Nazi symbols were torn down as people began to rebuild their shattered countries.

A soldier drags a Nazi flag behind him after the liberation of France

The German national emblem (*Hoheitsabzeichen*)

Swastika surrounded by oak-leaf wreath

Soviet soldier raises the Red Flag over the German capital, Berlin

Fall of Berlin
On May 2, 1945, two days after Hitler committed suicide, Soviet soldiers raised the Red Flag on top of the Reichstag (German parliament). It had taken two-and-a-half years to push the Germans back from Stalingrad to Berlin, the German capital.

The atomic bomb

Two German scientists split a uranium atom and caused a chain reaction of huge power in 1938. After the US entered the war in 1941, a team of scientists—many having fled Nazi Germany—turned this into a bomb. The Manhattan Project, based in Los Alamos, New Mexico, developed three bombs. The first was tested on July 16, 1945.

Enola Gay

This US Superfortress bomber dropped its load over Hiroshima, Japan, at 8:15 a.m. on August 6, 1945.

Powerful twin-propeller engines enabled B-29 to carry heavy loads over long distances

Small, but deadly

The 9,000-lb (4,082-kg) bomb (named "Little Boy") dropped on Hiroshima was 2,000 times more powerful than any other bomb.

"Little Boy" was 10 ft (3 m) long, with a diameter of 28 in (71 cm)

Bottle fused by blast

Hiroshima horror

"Little Boy" exploded 2,000 ft (600 m) above Hiroshima. It created a blinding heat flash and a blast that flattened 5 sq miles (13 sq km) of buildings. In five days, 138,661 people died.

Mushroom cloud visible 360 miles (580 km) away

Only a handful of brick buildings survived the blast at Nagasaki

Wind blasts outward at 500 mph (800 kph)

Survivors clutch emergency supplies of rice

Bombing of Nagasaki

On August 9, 1945, the final bomb was dropped on Nagasaki, Japan. "Fat Man" weighed 10,000 lb (4,536 kg). It was intended for Kokura, a military base, but poor weather meant Nagasaki was substituted at the last moment. About 73,884 people were killed and 51,000 buildings were damaged or totally destroyed.

Museum of Science and Industry has remained untouched since August 1945

Cloud rises to 33,000 ft (10,000 m)

"A shattering flash filled the sky… and the world collapsed around me."
A HIROSHIMA SURVIVOR

Survivors

More than 200,000 citizens of Hiroshima and Nagasaki were killed by the bombs. Many more suffered burns and injuries such as radiation sickness. The long-term effects of radiation, including cancer, on survivors and their future children makes it impossible to calculate the exact number of deaths.

Japan surrenders

On the same day as the Nagasaki bombing, the USSR invaded Manchuria, China. Japan's Supreme War Council met with Emperor Hirohito, but came up with no plan. Hirohito took charge and, on August 14, surrendered to the Allies, provided he could remain as emperor. His broadcast to the Japanese nation was the first time they ever heard his voice.

Japanese prisoners of war learn of their country's surrender

Temperature at ground level reaches 9,000°F (5,000°C)

Twice too often

Hiroshima and Nagasaki were rebuilt, but a gutted area of Hiroshima remains as a memorial to the horrors of atomic weapons. An international anti-nuclear conference meets annually in Hiroshima.

Victory

Front page news in Britain

The Germans' unconditional surrender, on May 7, 1945, in Rheims, France, was witnessed by representatives from each Ally (Britain, the US, France, and the USSR). It was repeated in Berlin on May 8— VE (Victory in Europe) Day. After the two atomic bombs, Japan surrendered formally on USS *Missouri* in Tokyo Bay on September 2, 1945. After six years of war, the world was at last at peace.

"East and west have met. This is the news for which the whole Allied world has been waiting. The forces of liberation have joined hands."

US RADIO COMMENTATOR, 1945

Fireworks over Moscow
Moscow celebrated with a fireworks display and military parade. Captured Nazi war trophies were laid at the Soviet leaders' feet.

St. George killing the dragon

Japan
VJ (Victory in Japan) Day, on August 15, 1945, was celebrated throughout the world, but many Japanese troops continued to fight. Peace was only finally established in September.

George Cross
First awarded by British king George VI in 1940 to those who showed heroism.

Cross of Valor
Polish servicemen who displayed great courage in battle were awarded the Cross of Valor.

Indian newspaper printed in English

VE day in New York

On May 8, the world could celebrate. Across the US, plus in Paris and other newly liberated European cities, people held street parties. In London, Prime Minister Winston Churchill appeared on the balcony of Buckingham Palace with the royal family to thousands of cheering people.

Ticker-tape streamers add to the party atmosphere in Wall Street, New York

The aftermath

The world faced a huge task in 1945. Both sides suffered terrible losses, with 55 million deaths. The USSR lost 20 million people; Poland, one-fifth of its people; and the Jews, six million. All countries, except the US, suffered ruined cities, factories, and farms. German and Japanese leaders were tried for war crimes, and their soldiers held in POW camps. Every country shared a strong desire never to relive the horrors of World War II.

United Nations
Representatives of 26 nations met in Washington, D.C., on January 1, 1942, and agreed not to make peace with the Axis without the other UN members. A permanent UN organization was established in October 1945, with 51 members.

Prefab housing
Prefabricated (ready-built) houses were used in Britain for the thousands of people made homeless by bombing. The prefabs came in kits and took a few days to construct. More than 150,000 were erected in the 1940s. Although intended as temporary structures, some survive today.

Rubble gangs
Across Germany, citizens cleared up their ruined towns and cities and helped in the reconstruction. The work was hard and unpleasant—workers often found bodies in cellars and basements.

Wreck of Hess's Messerschmitt Me110 fighter

Crash leads to prison
On May 10, 1941, Rudolf Hess, deputy leader of the Nazi Party, flew from Germany to Scotland. The plane crash-landed and Hess surrendered. The exact circumstances of Hess's flight have never been fully revealed.

War crimes trials

Many Nazi and Japanese officials stood trial for war crimes. At Nuremberg, Germany, 1945–46, a trial of 22 leading Nazis was organized by an International Military Tribunal; 12 were sentenced to death. In Japan, General Tojo was executed in 1948.

Peace park

This memorial stands in Peace Park in Hiroshima, a reminder of the terrible damage nuclear weapons can inflict. Since the war, peace campaigners around the world have protested to ensure that nuclear weapons are never again used in war.

Rationing continues

The end of the war did not end the shortages across Europe. Until farming and industry could return to normal production, food and basic essentials remained in short supply. Bread was rationed for the first time in Britain in 1946 and rationing of meat did not end until 1954.

British Ministry of Food ration book for 1949–50

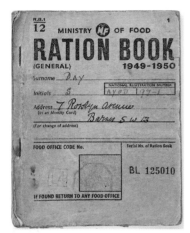

Affluent America

The US emerged stronger and richer than before the war. Except for its Pacific islands, no part of the US had been bombed or invaded. Its people now entered a time of full employment and rising wages, and many could afford new homes and cars.

Did you know?

BITE-SIZED FACTS

Some 29 amphibious Sherman tanks were launched from Allied ships on D-Day, but 27 sank in high seas. In 2000, divers located most of these tanks on the seabed.

In 1974, Japanese soldier Hiroo Onoda came out of the jungle of the Pacific island of Lubang after hiding there for 29 years, unaware that his country had surrendered.

Utility furniture was designed to use as little scarce raw materials as possible. It was available to newlyweds and families who had lost everything in an air raid.

The charity Oxfam was set up in 1942 to raise money for children in war-ravaged Greece. Today, the organization helps to relieve suffering all over the world.

In 2003, a message in a bottle washed up on a Swedish beach, sent 60 years earlier by an Estonian refugee hiding on Gotska Sandøen, 93 miles (150 km) away. Around 2,000 refugees from the Baltic states had found safety there during the war.

Where radio transmitters or telephones were unavailable, the military used carrier pigeons. Armies had special pigeon divisions with mobile pigeon pens.

Japan and the USSR never formally ended hostilities. An official peace treaty in 2000 came to nothing. Japan wanted Russia to return four offshore islands that it seized at the end of the war.

In 1939, Swiss chemist Paul Müller realized the chemical DDT works as an insecticide. Thanks to his discovery, DDT protected troops from insect-borne diseases in the war.

Princess Elizabeth (on the right)

Princess Elizabeth, later the UK's Queen Elizabeth II, did her part in the war. She joined the Auxiliary Territorial Service and drove a truck.

In 1935, the British government asked Robert Watson-Watt to work on a "death ray" to destroy enemy aircraft with radio waves. Instead, he used radio waves to detect incoming aircraft; radar (radio detection and ranging) was born.

A British soldier picks his demob shirt

On leaving the military, every British soldier received a set of civilian clothing: a "demobilization" suit, shirt, two shirt collars, a raincoat, hat, tie, two pairs of socks, and shoes.

Penicillin saved millions of soldiers' lives. It went into full-scale production in 1942.

Both sides used messenger dogs. The US army also trained platoons of war dogs. They served in the Pacific as scouts and sentries.

Members of the 8th Army Carrier Pigeon Service

Message brought by pigeon mail

A German soldier with his messenger dog

QUESTIONS AND ANSWERS

Sean Connery as 007 in the
first Bond film, *Dr. No* (1962)

Q Which wartime double agent was the inspiration for James Bond?

A Author Ian Fleming was impressed by Yugoslavian-born spy Dusko Popov, and based his character 007 on him. Abwehr (the German intelligence ageny) recruited Popov in 1940, but he was anti-Nazi and soon spying for MI5 and MI6 (British intelligence agencies). They supplied him with fake information for his Nazi bosses. Popov spoke five languages, had his own invisible ink formula, and was the first spy to use microdots (photos shrunk to dot size). In 1941, he went to the US. He obtained intelligence that the Japanese were planning an air strike on Pearl Harbor, but the FBI did not act on this. In the US, Popov lived in a penthouse apartment and went out with actresses, building a reputation for a playboy lifestyle. He wrote about his wartime activities in *Spy, Counterspy* (1974).

Q What did "Magic" do in the war?

A "Magic" was the codename for US cryptographers working on Japan's cipher Purple Machine, invented by Jinsaburo Ito in 1939. In September 1940, William Friedman cracked the code, leading to US success at the Battle of the Midway.

Q What secret code did American marines use?

A From 1942, US Marines in the Pacific used the Navajo language as their secret code. It is a complex language and few non-Navajo could speak it. The Navajo Indians had never needed military vocabulary, so existing words were given new meanings. About 400 Navajo Indians, the Code Talkers, were trained to use the code. The Japanese never cracked it.

Q Which side first used paratroopers?

A The Soviets were the first, which they showed to military observers in 1935. They helped the Germans train their own. The Allies caught up only in 1940—the Central Landing School opened near Manchester, England. Soldiers from all of the Allied nations trained there and within six months, nearly 500 of them were ready for action.

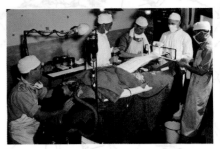

A soldier is given a blood transfusion
at an advanced dressing station

Q Which medical advance saved soldiers' lives?

A The biggest lifesaver was blood transfusion. Austrian-American doctor Karl Landsteiner had identified different blood groups in 1901, but more work was needed. World War II was the first major conflict in which blood transfusions saved many lives.

Q Which fighter planes had fangs?

A The RAF painted shark's teeth on Curtiss Kittyhawks, which they flew in North Africa. The fangs raised morale by making the pilots feel invincible. The Kittyhawk could carry one 500-lb (227-kg) bomb and was armed with six 0.5-in (12.7-mm) machine guns.

A paratrooper
on an exercise

Kittyhawks of No. 112
Squadron RAF, 1943

Timeline

World War II was fought on many different fronts and this timeline highlights some key moments to give a picture of wartime history as it happened. Unfortunately, there is not enough space here to list every major event of the war, so many milestones have had to be omitted.

German soldiers march into Poland, 1939

1939

SEPTEMBER 1
Germany invades Poland.

SEPTEMBER 3
Britain and France declare war on Germany.

SEPTEMBER 27
Polish Warsaw surrenders to Germany.

SEPTEMBER 28
Germany and USSR divide up Poland.

NOVEMBER 30
The USSR invades Finland.

1940

APRIL–MAY
Germany invades Denmark, Norway, the Netherlands, Belgium, Luxembourg, and France.

MAY 26–JUNE 4
Operation Dynamo evacuates 338,000 Allied troops from Dunkirk, France.

JUNE 10
Italy declares war on Britain and France.

JUNE 14
German troops enter Paris, France.

JUNE 21
France surrenders and Germany governs northern France.

JULY 10
The Battle of Britain begins.

SEPTEMBER 7
Germany bombs British cities.

SEPTEMBER 12
Italy invades Egypt.

SEPTEMBER 27
The Axis sign the Tripartite Pact.

OCTOBER 12
Battle of Britain ends.

Japan attacks Pearl Harbor, 1941

1941

JANUARY 22
British and Australian troops capture Tobruk, Libya.

MARCH 1
Bulgaria joins the Axis.

APRIL 5
Germany invades Yugoslavia and Greece.

MAY 27
The British sink the *Bismarck*.

JUNE 22
Germany invades the USSR.

SEPTEMBER 15
The Siege of Leningrad begins.

DECEMBER 7
Japan attacks Pearl Harbor and starts to invade Malaya.

DECEMBER 8
Britain and US declare war on Japan.

DECEMBER 11
Germany declares war on the US.

DECEMBER 25
Hong Kong surrenders to the Japanese.

Identification letters

Exhausts behind the propeller

A Hawker Hurricane, used by the RAF in the Battle of Britain, 1940

Target symbol on wing

The Germans in North Africa, 1942

1942

FEBRUARY 15
The Japanese capture Singapore.

MARCH
First prisoners at Auschwitz, Poland, are gassed.

APRIL 28–MAY 8
The US halts Japanese advance at the Battle of Coral Sea.

JUNE 4–6
The US defeats the Japanese at the Battle of the Midway.

AUGUST 19
The battle for the Soviet city of Stalingrad begins.

OCTOBER 23–NOVEMBER 4
Britain defeats Germany at El Alamein, North Africa.

NOVEMBER 8
US and British troops land in northwest Africa.

1943

JANUARY 31
The German army is defeated at Stalingrad.

FEBRUARY 8
The US captures Guadacanal from the Japanese.

APRIL 19
Nazi troops attack the Warsaw ghetto in Poland.

MAY 12
The German army in North Africa surrenders.

JULY 9
Allied troops invade Sicily, Italy.

JULY 25
Benito Mussolini is overthrown.

SEPTEMBER 3
Allied troops invade mainland Italy. As a result, Italy surrenders.

OCTOBER 13
Italy declares war on Germany.

1944

JANUARY 27
The Siege of Leningrad ends.

MARCH 8
Japan attempts an invasion of India.

JUNE 6
D-Day: Allied forces land in Normandy, France, and press inland.

US troops in the Philippines, 1944

Benito Mussolini

AUGUST 25
The Allies liberate Paris.

OCTOBER 17
US troops land in the Philippines.

1945

MARCH 7
British and US troops cross the Rhine River, Germany.

APRIL 30
Adolf Hitler commits suicide.

MAY 7
Germany unconditionally surrenders.

MAY 8
VE (Victory in Europe) Day.

AUGUST 6
The US drops "Little Boy" atomic bomb on Hiroshima, Japan.

AUGUST 9
The US drops "Fat Man" atomic bomb on Nagasaki, Japan.

AUGUST 15
VJ (Victory in Japan) Day, following Japan's surrender.

OCTOBER 24
Permanent United Nations (UN) is founded.

Find out more

You may be able to hear about the war firsthand from older generations of your family. Personal accounts are also online and in books. Many war museums have interactive displays that bring wartime to life and TV documentaries show footage of the war. Finally, movies have dramatized almost every wartime experience.

Cabinet War Rooms
In London, you can visit the underground Cabinet War Rooms where Prime Minister Churchill and his War Cabinet met from 1940 until the end of the war. The rooms are just as they were during the war.

Monument at Murmansk
Every country that was in World War II has memorials that remember the dead, such as this concrete statue of a Soviet soldier, known as "Aloysha," which symbolizes the USSR's war heroes.

D-Day anniversary
Anniversaries of wartime events, such as D-Day, are a chance to reflect and find out more about your country's history.

War museums
World War II collections in museums are still expanding, as more artefacts come to light. The Imperial War Museum North in Manchester, UK, displays a large collection.

Imperial War Museum North

DELEGATE CAR PARK

War movies

Films express not only the horrors of war, but also stories of individual bravery. *Schindler's List* (1993) dramatizes the true story of a German businessman, Oskar Schindler, who saved hundreds of Jews by employing them in his factory.

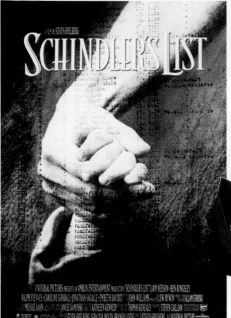

Film poster of *Schindler's List*

The menorah is an important symbol of Judaism

Holocaust memorial

Many memorials honor those who died in Nazi death camps. This memorial at Mauthausen, Austria, is shaped like a *menorah* (candlestick).

Caught on film

One of the most gripping tales of the Resistance is the 1964 film, *The Train*. French railroad worker Labiche tries to sabotage a Nazi train smuggling art out of Paris before liberation.

USEFUL WEBSITES

- Explore WWII facts, battles, photos, videos, and more: **www.history.com/topics/world-war-ii**
- The Smithsonian site contains an introductory movie and historic images and artifacts: **www.americanhistory.si.edu**
- National Geographic site remembering World War II: **www.education.nationalgeographic.com**
- A multimedia resource about the Holocaust: **www.history.com/topics/world-war-ii/the-holocaust**

Omaha beach D-Day memorial

The inscription reads: "The Allied forces landing on this shore which they call Omaha Beach liberate Europe—June 6th 1944."

Places to visit

**NATIONAL WORLD WAR II MEMORIAL
WASHINGTON, D.C.**

- The memorial honors the 16 million who served in the armed forces of the US, the more than 400,000 who died, and all who supported the war effort at home.

**PEARL HARBOR
OAHU, HAWAII**

- The battleships on view mark the beginning and end of the war for the US.

**NATIONAL D-DAY MUSEUM
NEW ORLEANS, LOUISIANA**

- The most comprehensive US WWII museum, this superb museum covers more than 125 amphibious assaults carried out by American soldiers across Europe and the Pacific.

**INTREPID SEA-AIR-SPACE MUSEUM
NEW YORK, NEW YORK**

- This indestructible aircraft carrier fought in the Battle of Leyte Gulf, Philippines, and withstood five kamikaze strikes.

**NATIONAL MUSEUM OF THE PACIFIC WAR
FREDERICKSBURG, TEXAS**

- The only museum in the continental US dedicated exclusively to the Pacific War features innovative displays and engaging walk-through dioramas.

**MUSEUM OF WORLD WAR II
BOSTON, MASSACHUSETTS**

- The collection houses 6,000 artifacts, including original uniforms.

English translation of the French inscription, which appears above

69

Glossary

AIR RAID A bomb attack from the air.

AIR-RAID SHELTER A place that afforded protection from the bombing during an air raid.

ALLIANCE A group of allies who have agreed to act in cooperation; they often set out shared goals in an official treaty.

AMMUNITION Bullets and shells.

AMPHIBIOUS Operate on land and water.

ANTIAIRCRAFT GUN A gun with enough range to fire at enemy aircraft.

ANTI-SEMITIC Holding views that discriminate against and persecute Jews.

German airmen making up ammunition belts

ARMISTICE End of hostilities.

ATOMIC BOMB A powerful weapon that uses nuclear fission—the splitting of an atom from a radioactive element.

ATROCITY An appalling, wicked act.

AUXILIARY Describes someone providing help or backup.

AXIS The name of the alliance of Germany, Italy, and their allies.

BARRAGE BALLOON A tethered balloon, strung with cables, used to obstruct low-flying aircraft.

BLOOD TRANSFUSION Injecting blood from a donor into the veins of a patient who is losing blood.

BUNKER An underground bomb shelter.

CAMOUFLAGE Coloring and patterns designed to blend in with the background.

CIPHER A code that substitutes letters or symbols by a set key.

COMMUNIST A supporter of communism—a belief system that opposes the free market and aims for a classless society.

CONCENTRATION CAMP A prison camp for non-military prisoners. At Nazi concentration camps, prisoners included Jews, eastern Europeans, and other groups considered to be enemies of the state.

CONVOY Merchant ships traveling together, protected by a naval escort.

CRYPTOGRAPHER Someone who studies, creates, or deciphers codes.

CRYPTOGRAPHY The study and creation of secret codes.

DEMOBILIZATION Dispersing troops after active service.

DEMOCRATIC Based on the principles of democracy, where government representatives are elected by the people.

DICTATOR A ruler who takes total control, without giving the people a say.

ESPIONAGE Spying.

EVACUATE Move away from danger.

EVACUEE Someone who has been moved from a place of danger.

FASCIST A supporter of fascism—a belief system opposed to democracy and in favor of a powerful, armed state.

A Gurkha in jungle camouflage, Malaya

FIELD TELEPHONE A portable military telephone.

FUSELAGE The body of an airplane.

GAS In the context of war, a poisonous gas used to harm or kill the enemy. All sides had supplies in World War II, but it was never deployed as a weapon.

GAS CHAMBER An enclosure where people were exterminated using gas.

GAS MASK A breathing device that gives protection from a gas attack.

GESTAPO Nazi secret police service.

GHETTO An area of a city where a particular racial group is confined.

GRENADE A small bomb that is hurled by hand.

HOLOCAUST The mass murder of millions of Jews and others by the Nazis during World War II.

Field telephone

IMPERIAL To do with an empire or emperor.

INCENDIARY Describes a bomb, bullet, or other device designed to cause fire.

INFANTRY Foot soldiers.

INTELLIGENCE Useful military or political information, or the spies who gather it.

LAND GIRL A young woman who worked to help the war effort, usually on farms to produce food. Women were also put to work producing other valuable resources, from raw materials to weaponry and parachutes.

Locating a target for an antiaircraft gun

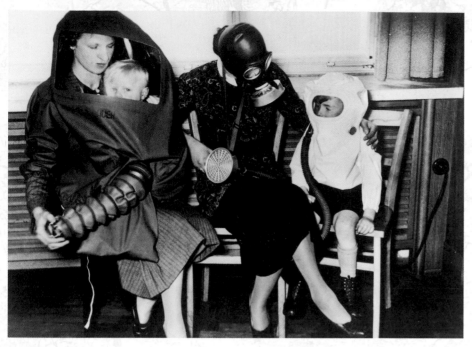

German gas mask designs, 1939

RADAR "Radio Detection and Ranging." A detection system that uses radio waves to locate objects.

RADIATION SICKNESS Illness caused by exposure to radioactivity.

RATIONING Restricting provisions, such as food, in a time of scarcity.

REFUGEE Someone forced to flee their country in search of safety.

RESISTANCE An organization opposed to an occupying enemy force, especially the European groups that sabotaged the Nazis during their occupation of Europe.

SABOTAGE A deliberate action designed to destroy or disrupt.

SHELL An explosive device that is fired, for example, from a cannon.

SURRENDER To give up control.

LIBERATION Freeing from occupation.

MACHINE GUN An automatic gun that fires bullets in rapid succession.

MINE (1) An underground chamber packed with explosives. (2) A bomb laid on the ground that detonates when traveled over. (3) A floating bomb in the sea for destroying ships and submarines.

MINESWEEPER A ship that drags the water to find undersea mines.

MORALE Strength of purpose, confidence, or faith.

Young women working at a sawmill

MORSE CODE A code where each letter of the alphabet is represented by dots and dashes.

MORTAR BOMB A heavy bomb, usually fired from a tank.

NATIONALIST Someone who believes in nationalism—the belief in the importance and dominance of their own nation state.

OCCUPATION The time when an enemy force takes over a country.

PARATROOPER A soldier air-dropped into territory, wearing a parachute.

PARTISAN A member of a resistance movement working in enemy-occupied territory.

PENICILLIN A mold extract that prevents bacteria growth. Its antibacterial properties were discovered by Alexander Fleming in 1928. By 1942, penicillin was available to treat soldiers with infections.

POW "Prisoner of War." Someone captured in wartime. Mostly members of the armed forces.

PROPAGANDA Information intended to convince people of a particular viewpoint. It may take the form of posters, broadcasts, or air-dropped leaflets, for example.

Alexander Fleming with a petri dish of penicillin

SWASTIKA An ancient symbol—a cross with each arm bent at a right angle—adopted by the Nazis as their emblem.

TORPEDO A self-propelled underwater missile, fired from a boat or submarine.

TREATY A formal agreement between nations.

U-BOAT A German submarine.

ULTIMATUM A final demand that if it is not met will result in serious consequences and a total breakdown of communication.

UTILITY Describes clothing, household objects, or furniture produced in wartime Britain under the Utility Scheme. All Utility items were designed to waste as little as possible, in terms of both raw materials and the manufacturing process.

Index

Acknowledgments

Dorling Kindersley would like to thank:
Terry Charman, Mark Seaman, Mark Pindelski, Elizabeth Bowers, Neil Young, Christopher Dowling, Nigel Steel, Mike Hibberd, Alan Jeffreys, Paul Cornish, & the photography archive team at the Imperial War Museum for their help; Sheila Collins & Simon Holland for design & editorial assistance; Samantha Nunn, Marie Osborne, & Amanda Russell for additional picture research; Chris Bernstein for the index; the author for assisting with revisions; Claire Bowers, David Ekholm-Jalbum, Sunita Gahir, Joanne Little, Nigel Ritchie, Susan St. Louis, & Bulent Yusuf for the clipart; David Ball, Neville Graham, Rose Horridge, Joanne Little, & Susan Nicholson for the wallchart; BCP, Marianne Petrou, & Owen Peyton Jones for checking the digitized files.

For this edition, the publishers would also like to thank: Niki Foreman for text editing and Carron Brown for proofreading.

The publishers would like to thank the following for their kind permission to reproduce their photographs:
a=above, b=below, c=center, f=far, l=left, r=right, t=top

Advertising Archives: 51bc, 63clb. Airbourne Forces Museum, Aldershot: 32–33. AKG London: 45cra, 51t; German Press Corps 13tc. The Art Archive: 30cr. Camera Press: 7br; Imperial War Museum 53tr. Charles Fraser Smith: 26cra. Corbis: 33tl, 40c, 59br, 66tl; Bettmann 54–55b, 61, 64–65, 66cra, 67tr; Owen Franken 69br; Hulton Deutsch Collections 20cl, 31tr, 53tc, 62c; Richard Klune 68b; Carmen Redondo 52–53; David Samuel Robbins 63r; Michael St Maur Sheil 69ca; Sygma/ Orban Thierry 68cl; Yogi, Inc 68cr. D-Day Museum, Portsmouth: 54cla. Eden Camp Modern History Theme Museum, Malton: 22cl, 29tr, 36bl, 60bl, 62cr, 63cl. HK Melton: 16c, 17cla, 17c, 26bl, 26br, 28crb, 31tl, 31cl. Hoover Institution: Walter

Leschander 28cb. **Hulton Archive/Getty Images:** 8cl, 8bl, 10cl, 14cr, 16tt, 17tl, 23tl, 26crb, 38b, 39cl, 39br 43tc, 56b, 57c, 57br; © AFF/AFS, Amsterdam, The Netherlands 37tr; Alexander Ustinov 60cl; Fox Photos 20bl, 66cb, 68–69; Keystone 12tc, 14b, 15tl, 25tc; Keystone Features 28ca, 29b; Reg Speller 36br; US Army Signal Corps Photograph 53cr. **Imperial War Museum:** Dorling Kindersley Picture Library 16br, 26cl, 26c, 26cr, 37tl, 45cr, 70cr; IWM Photograph Archive 11cr (ZZZ9182C), 21cr (HU1185), 21tr (HL5181), 22tr (HU635), 23tr (CH1277), 24cl (B5501), 34cr (TR1253), 34bl (D18056), 35bl (IND1492), 40br (IND3468), 41cr (C4989), 44t (RUS2109), 48cl (E14582), 50cr (C494), 56c (BU1292), 56cr (6352), 64tr (TR1581), 64c (H41668), 64bl (TR2572), 64br (STT39), 65tr (TR2410), 65cr (TR50), 65b (TR975), 67tl (STT853), 67br (NYF40310), 70tr (FE250), 70cl (MH5559), 70bc (TR330), 71tl (HU39759), 71cr (TR1468), 71bl (TR910). **Kobal Collection:** Amblin/Universal 69tl; United Artists 65tl, 69cl; Universal 48cra. **Mary Evans Picture Library:** 9br. **M.O.D Michael Jenner Photography:** 61. **Pattern Room, Nottingham:** 47b. **National Cryptological Museum:** 31cr. **National Maritime Museum, London:** 42–43c. **Novosti:** 46cr, 46bl, 47tl, 47cl; 45t. **Oesterreichische**

Nationalbibliothek: 9tl. **Peter Newark's Pictures:** 6cr, 8tl, lttr, 12–13t, 13b, 15cra, 17bl, 18c, 19bc, 19br, 22c, 25cl, 26cl, 31br, 32clb, 34tr, 35br, 36tl, 37b, 41b, 47tr, 50b, 51bl, 52bl, 55cr, 58tr, 58–59; Yevgnei Khaldei 57bc. **Popperfoto:** 17cra, 29cr, 34br, 35tl. **Public Record Office Picture Library:** 26cla, 30crb. **Robert Harding Picture Library:** 59tr. **Robert Hunt Library:** 22–23b. **Ronald Grant Archive:** British Lion Films 12b. **Royal Air Force Museum, Hendon:** 26cla. **Royal Signals Museum, Blandford Camp:** 55tr. **Topham Picturepoint:** 9cl, 29cl, 41cla, 43cra, 48tr, 49tl, 49tr, 50cl, 51br, 52tr, 52c, 53br, 63tl; Press Association 41tr; Universal Pictorial Press 68tr. **Trh Pictures:** 24bl, 32tr, 37tc, 38c, 55tl, 55c; Imperial War Museum 33tc; Leszek Erenfeicht 8–9; National Archives 24–25b, 39t; United Nations 58br; US NA 54tr; US National Archives 42clb. **Weimar Archive:** 9cr.

All other images © Dorling Kindersley
For further information see
www.dkimages.com